A Patriot's American Dream

Building a Legacy of Purpose, Perseverance, and Positivity

Tim J. Smith Sr., Sergeant (Ret)

Book written by Tim J. Smith Sr., Sergeant (Ret)

chapters
Contributing writing by Dan Curran, Co-Founder of Chapters

Cover and book layout by Rosanna Cerutti
Editing by Charles Dayton, Rebekah Icenesse, and Astrid Zeppenfeld

Manufactured in the United States of America.

PUBLISHING CONCEPTS LLC

For more information, please contact:
Publishing Concepts LLC
6590 Scanlan Avenue
St. Louis, MO 63139
www.PublishingConceptsLLC.com

PAPERBACK ISBN: 978-1-957307-79-4
EBOOK (PDF) ISBN: 978-1-957307-80-0

PERSONAL MEMOIRS

1 2 3 4 5 6 7 8 9 10

Tim with his wife, Terri, and their sons, Timmy Jr. (right) and Tyler, on November 10, 2024.

A Patriot's American Dream

Building a Legacy of Purpose, Perseverance, and Positivity

Table of Contents

Introduction

A Patriot's American Dream is a compelling memoir that traces Timothy J. Smith Sr.'s remarkable journey from the basketball courts of St. Louis to the battlefields of Iraq, and ultimately to the helm of a successful veteran-employing business. This inspiring narrative doesn't shy away from the harsh realities of war, the invisible wounds of PTSD, or the daunting challenges of recurring cancer. Instead, it showcases how these obstacles became steppingstones on Smith's path (and yours!) to personal growth and entrepreneurial success.

Interwoven throughout these experiences is Smith's hard-fought battle with cancer. His resilience in the face of this recurring illness offers powerful lessons on maintaining hope and determination in the most challenging circumstances.

The book is rich with themes that will resonate with a wide audience, especially veterans who desire to become entrepreneurs:

- The impact of military service and the transition back to civilian life
- Strategies for coping with and healing from PTSD
- The challenges and rewards of veteran-focused entrepreneurship
- Resilience in the face of health challenges
- The importance of education and lifelong learning
- The role of family and support systems in overcoming life's obstacles
- Leadership lessons from military service applied to business
- Redefining success and the American Dream

Readers should feel empowered to face their own challenges with renewed strength and perspective. They'll have gained insights into:

- Managing PTSD and other mental health issues more effectively
- Approaching health challenges with resilience and a positive mindset
- Starting or growing a business, particularly one that benefits their community

- Finding purpose and meaning in life, regardless of past experiences
- Building and maintaining strong support networks
- Giving back to their communities and helping others facing similar challenges

Tim carries a profound gratitude for the people who have stood by him—his brothers and sisters in arms, the veterans he's dedicated his life to serving, and the family who inspires him every day. Through each trial—on the battlefield, in hospital rooms, and in the quietest moments of doubt—he has been guided by an unwavering belief in something greater than himself. His story is more than just his own; it's a tribute to everyone who has struggled, endured, and found the strength to rise again. To Tim, life is a precious gift, one meant to be lived boldly and shared openly. And he believes, with all his heart, that no matter how dark the road may seem, there is always light just ahead.

1

Beginnings: Foundations of a Patriot

Roots of Resilience: Family, Faith, and Early Lessons

February 13, 2016

Life is sure funny how it works out sometimes. I am starting to write this book because of some health issue that I am having right now. About 12 days ago, I started having a really bad cough; it is February in St. Louis, MO, so it is pretty cold outside. I started to take the Z-Pak after my appointment and started feeling better for about seven days. About five days ago, I started coughing again very badly and my chest started hurting. Little did I know how these seemingly trivial symptoms were the start of one heck of a journey. But, before I speak of this journey, let's take a step back.

I was in the Army from June 26, 2003 to February 18, 2007. Before I was deployed to Iraq, around January 3, 2004, I had pneumonia in my right lung. I remember the medic in Baumholder, Germany, telling me before I deployed to keep an eye out for pneumonia in the future because once you have been exposed to it, it is easier to catch. For some reason, the medic saying that has always stuck in my mind. I went to the Southwest Medical Center and explained what I was feeling. They explained that we better get an x-ray done, just to make sure everything was good. Two days later, I went to get the x-ray done and they explained that I may have a nodule on the right side of my lung. I really had no idea what that means and, honestly, I was a little nervous. They explained to me the best next step is to get the CAT scan done.

I followed the doctor's orders and ended up at Total Access Urgent Care. Before they started to run the CT, they had a paramedic come take some blood. He was a younger guy like me, probably about 35 or so. We started talking. He was in the Marine Corps and was over in Iraq the same time I was there and that gave me a sense of calm. I asked about the nodule and what it could be. He explained a few things, but, more than anything, what made me feel comfortable was interacting with someone who had probably experienced some of the similar situations that I did.

After they ran the CAT scan, they explained that I had a nodule that was two centimeters big on my right lung. They clarified that if it is one centimeter or more, they suggest seeing a pulmonologist. I have the pulmonologist appointment in three days. It is all coming back to me now—the fear of the unknown. I remember feeling the same way before enlisting in the Army in 2003. I had no idea what to expect then and I have no idea what to expect now. I do know that many things have changed since those carefree days of being a younger man with no sense of direction. I am fortunate—I have been married for 11 years to my beautiful wife, Terri. We have been best friends for 17 years. It took me over six years to finally win her over, but with a lot of maturing and wooing her, I was able to marry my dream girl. I am also extremely lucky because she has blessed me with the two greatest boys in the world: Timmy Jr., who at the time of this writing is ten years old, and Tyler, who is seven years old. I really did not know the true meaning of happiness as an adult before I was married and had my own children. I would just tell my boys, "Anything you want bad enough, keep fighting for it and don't give up. Look at how long it took your mother to finally take me seriously."

The way I feel now sitting in this office is like having butterflies before a big game. I am nervous about going to the pulmonologist, but I know I have to face this head on. I will read the test results now and there are the three different options: 1) If your nodule proves to be benign, continue to follow up over the next five years. 2) If the tests cannot tell if your nodule is benign or malignant, then surgery may be advised. 3) If your tests show your nodule is definitely malignant, surgery probably will be advised. I am hoping and praying that everything will be okay and at this time, as I am writing this on a note pad I just bought, I have no idea. I truly do believe in positive thinking though and believe I will get through this.

A few months ago, I remember my dad and I were driving because we were doing some quality inspections on some of the buildings that we clean. He told me I may want to write some of this down because it had been some pretty amazing experiences I never could have imagined. I kind of blew him off and said one day I might, but I don't have time right now. I guess one thing I learned at an early age is that life can be cut short. I mostly wanted to write this for my two young sons, wife, parents, and anybody else who believes in the American Dream.

Lessons from the Court: Basketball and Building Character

I know it seems like I am repeating myself here a little bit, but I am going to explain how my mom, dad, and basketball taught me some life lessons. Up until I was about nine years old, I had a very bad speech impediment where I had trouble pronouncing my "s"es. My mom started taking me to a speech therapist in Kindergarten. She always wanted to make sure that I had everything I needed to be successful in school. I was always a pretty shy kid and I really hated doing any type of school activity where I had to talk in front of people. I remember my speech therapist would put a brown paper bag on a chair. Whenever I would pronounce a word correctly, I was able to shoot a ball into the bag. Apparently, after that exercise, I found something that really motivated me to work on my speech. My mom never gave up on me, no matter how much I wanted to give up on myself and school. I am sure she gets a kick seeing me speak in public now because she has seen me at my worst, where I never wanted anyone to hear me speak. I am very thankful to my mom for that because today, I speak to my team members every day on different objectives that need to be met.

I am Irish and Italian, and it was very important for my mom and dad to sacrifice so my sister and I could get a Catholic education in grade school—at St. George in Affton, Missouri. Both of my parents worked very hard and saved money to make that happen for us. I must admit, it was a great community that was very tight-knit. Some of my mom's and dad's best friends went there and they all still keep in touch. The community consisted of a good number of blue-collar workers and very close families. I played basketball with the third-grade team because my birthday is July 29 and I started school a little bit late. My dad was a great basketball coach. He led us to four league championships in a row and we won three South County CYC championships. He was very tough on me in basketball because he knew that I could take it and had the potential. My dad would work from about 5 a.m. at the bakery until about 3 p.m. so he could coach our team on Tuesdays and Thursdays from 4 p.m. to 5:30 p.m. at the bakery warehouse. He stressed the importance of teamwork and how good defense wins a game. We never really had a one-star player, but five or six good players and two decent subs that knew their role and got the job done. He instilled in me hard work, for nothing will ever be given to you—you will have to earn it. We had some great times traveling in between the games and just talking. I have always looked up to my dad for honest advice. Even at times when I disagreed with him, I would listen, file it in my memory bank, and then make my own decision.

We would have some great basketball games at Mathilda Park. There was about an 80% chance you could find me there with my buddies: Dave Silva, his brother Sal, and Kirk Richmever. When I was about nine years old, we moved there and lived on Welmering, which was great because it was right by the park and I would walk up there every day I was at home. We would play there about four hours a day, relentlessly running games back and forth. It was a great part of my childhood because we would just hoop all day and night. Another thing I liked about playing sports was that it teaches you to win and lose. You are not going to win every time and that is okay. You learn how to deal with temporary failure and how you have the next game to improve and try to win. In life, not everything is going to go as planned. You have to adapt and overcome.

I went to Affton High School from 1994 to 1997. I had a very good time there, but I did not apply myself very hard when it came to academics. I really wish I would have, because if you don't have good grades, it really limits your college opportunities. I stayed eligible for basketball all four years and Coach Parker would always follow up with me about my grades. I remember in a few interviews he did about me in high school, he called me a gym rat because I was always working on my game.

I ended up averaging about 19.8 PPG my senior year and we had a decent season with about 16 wins and 11 loses; it was something like that. From that season and my junior season, I was fortunate to be invited to a five-star basketball camp in Pittsburgh, PA. I remember my junior year; I went to the camp with Chris Carrawell, who ended up playing at Duke, and Loren Wood, who ended up playing at Arizona and then professional ball overseas. The competition was great there and it was an awesome experience—playing in front of coaches like Norm Stewart from Mizzou, Jim Boheim from Syracuse, and Rick Pitino, who at the time was at Kentucky. It was funny because all the blue chip players had the opportunity and had their own room at Robert Morris College while all the regular players stayed two guys to a room. It reminded me of the old movie *Blue Chips* that Shaquille O'Neal starred in.

My experience in high school basketball was very positive; the rest was not as much. I have to take ownership of that though and I really did not try as hard as I could have. I was the kid sitting in the back of class just skating by. I did not really care about my grades. Truth be told, if I had not gotten a full ride to a junior college for basketball, I would not have attended. I remember one time after gym class, one of my gym teachers said in front of the entire class, "Mr. Smith, it is people like you that bring my property value down." I did not say anything as the class chuckled and laughed. I just thought to myself, "We will see about that one day."

I have always been a pretty quiet person, but inside, in my heart, I was remembering and thought to myself, "We will see one day." One thing I would tell any young child or teenager is that you have to think in high regards of yourself. I know, some of my friends and I did not think much of ourselves because other people did not think much of us. It is like a self-fulfilling prophecy. I would encourage any parent or schoolteacher to encourage their kids and tell them anything is possible. My mom and dad always encouraged me and believed in me. However, I did not believe in myself and it reflected in the way I carried myself.

I squeaked by in high school and graduated from Affton High School in 1997. In 1998, I obtained a full ride to Forest Park Community College and played basketball there for two years, and then I received a basketball scholarship to St. Mary's College in Leavenworth, Kansas. I only stayed one semester and then moved back to St. Louis. It was a very cool experience living in a college dorm; maybe too much fun, so back home to the STL I came.

2

Turning Points and Choices

Drifting and Direction: The Quest for Identity

The only thing I was really good at was coming to an end and I was lost. I was always identified as the white boy who was slow and could not jump but could score a lot of points at will. I kept asking myself, "What am I going to do now?"

I started attending University of Missouri, St. Louis (UMSL). I moved in with my Aunt Mo, who at the time, was living in South City off Arsenal Street. Aunt Mo is my mom's sister and has always been like my second mom to me. Aunt Mo obtained her Master's in Social Work and has been a social worker for over 30 years. I decided to follow her footsteps as a social worker. That was my major. I think my experience going to the Boys' Club of St. Louis always made me appreciate people that wanted to help out their community. I grew up going there from eight years old to 17 years old, so I was exposed to many races, cultures, and a lot of shit-talking. I had the experience of listening to groups like Public Enemy, LL COOL J, Ice Cube, 2 Pac, and many other great rappers at that time in the late 80s and early 90s. I also was exposed to many hard rock bands like Guns N Roses, Metallica, Mötley Crüe, Poison, and other great hair band music. I learned to adapt to both environments because I lived in both of them daily. I had a great time going there and the counselors there really shaped my life. I always looked up to them because they really cared about the boys. I had counselors like Larry Lichefski and Keith Czapla that were really good basketball players in their days and would coach us. One of my favorite counselors was named Bob Gummersbach. I played for Bob for two years with the Mini Supers and he taught me to throw the ball off the wall, catch it, pump fake, and then drain a jump shot. Bob was one of the nicest guys around but had a thunderous voice when he would yell at us. He would say, "Hey, Jack get over here" and you would hear it echo through the whole gym. Unfortunately, when I was 13 years old, Bob was at the St. Margaret of Scotland fish fry in South St. Louis. He told some young kid to stop messing with the fish fry sign. It was the early 90s and gangs were a pretty big thing around that time. As part of an initiation, some kid shot Bob and killed him. I am sure that shocked me when I was younger and I was like, "Damn, the world can be a cold place. One of the nicest guys that cared about people so much was gone so young." I believe that Bob was in his early 30s and about to get married. He was volunteering for Meals On Wheels and trying to get the elderly people some food. I was lucky enough to have a great mom and dad, but a lot of the guys I grew up with only had one parent, so I always felt very fortunate to have both my parents. The volunteers there helped many of us out and I wanted to do the same thing.

When I was not working, I worked as a lot attendant (cart pusher) at the Home Depot off of Hanley Road. About five of my buddies worked there in different departments, and it was a job where I could work about 30 hours and still go to my classes. I remember when I was not going to school or working, I could be found at the neighborhood pub having a few cocktails and shooting darts. I was pretty lost in that time of my life. I had no identity and really not a lot of self-confidence. I have heard many athletes feel like this when they are washed up and not playing the game anymore.

I ended up working at AWI trucking, changing truck tires on 18 wheelers and stacking pallets on the deck where the trucks would back in. It was one of the dirtiest jobs I have ever had. I remember some of the guys I worked with were so much faster at changing those tires compared to myself. I worked there for about a year and figured that was not my calling. I figured maybe I should keep looking.

The next job I had was at Nick's Irish Pub downtown. I was hired as a barback and worked Thursday, Friday, and Saturday night. I am 75% Irish and 25% Italian, so I thought that was a pretty cool experience. On Thursday and Saturday, an Irish band would perform and there was a two-dollar cover charge. I would collect the cover charge, check IDs, clean the tables, and restock the beer for the bartenders. I worked there for about a year and a half while going to school and doing my practicum for social work at the North Side Community Center, working with children with a very low socioeconomic status.

I would get off work around 4 a.m. and would have to be at the Center at 8 a.m. That practicum was very important to me because the children from five to 15 years old really counted on us. The kids that went there were really disadvantaged. I was humbled by the experience. That being said, they were always very happy to get positive reinforcement and I learned a lot from them.

In 2002, I had about 12 hours before I graduated from UMSL with my Bachelor's in Social Work. I spoke to Charlie Nash, who was one of the legends at the Boys Club of St. Louis. When we were kids, we thought he was larger than life because you heard so many stories about him. I spoke to him and he explained that he would be happy to have me join the staff there. I worked as a junior staff member in the summertime, from the age of 12 to the age of 14. I really enjoyed working there as a junior staff member and figured that this could be a good fit for me as a career.

It was the wintertime; I remember my friend Ray Atkison was killed in a car accident getting on the highway. Little Ray was two years younger than me and went to high school with me. He was always smiling, and I remember that, for a white boy, he could jump. He had a great personality and many friends that still remember him to this day. The night of his wake at Kutis, a lot of us went to a little bar in South St. Louis on Gravois by the Viaduct, by the old Wonder Bread store. We were all very young adults—between 19 and 26 years old. With alcohol and emotions running high at that age, it could have been a recipe for disaster—and it was. I remember a huge fight breaking out in the bar that led outside on Gravois Ave, a very busy street. There were probably about 20 people fighting. People just were talking smack and it led to a brawl. It was very irresponsible, and we were fighting because of emotions mixed with alcohol. Cars actually had to stop for a few minutes because the street was filled with people scrapping and throwing punches. A few minutes afterwards, my buddies Tim Lindsey, Matt Russo, and Frank Payne jumped in my car. There was this one guy still talking stuff and my buddy wanted to confront him. We followed him to Gravois and Dahlia. He called up one of his own buddies and they came outside. Luckily, I parked my car on Terrace because Dahlia is a one-way street. We got out of the car and walked toward the house. The guy's friend's dad came out with a shotgun. I remember telling my buddies, "Watch out because this guy has some heat," which is another word for gun. We were in the middle of the street and my buddy Tim was on the sidewalk, walking toward the guy. The guy fired the first round at the ground in our direction. I ran toward Tim and told him we had to get out of there. He took a few steps forward and the guy fired another round. A few of the BBs got him in the shin. You could see in his khaki pants the pepper spray from the shotgun shell. To be honest, Tim is probably one of the best street fighters I witnessed in South St. Louis.

We jogged up the street towards my car and an old guy about 70 years old came out and spoke to us for about one minute. I don't know many people that come outside to talk to a few kids that were just in an altercation and someone had just fired a few rounds at them. The older gentleman talked to us about how we needed to find God or find some sense of purpose. None of us really said anything and kind of laughed it off. Do you remember when I was eight years old and said I lived with my grandma and grandpa Smith for a while, along with my mom, dad, and sister? That was one block away from Gravois and Rosa where we lived with them as kids for a while and celebrated many birthdays, Christmases, Halloweens, and other occasions with all my family members. I remember driving down Rosa, driving past the house and thinking to myself, what am I doing with my life?

The next morning, we buried Ray at the cemetery and saw a good amount of the people we were fighting. Everything was good that day, and everyone was shaking hands and good to go. I remember when we were younger, sometimes it was like that. We would get into a fight the day before, and the next night, we were having a beer. A lot of it was immaturity and it was all pretty stupid looking back at it now. Live and learn. I just chalk it up as a learning experience.

That night, I kept replaying in my mind and thinking that maybe it was a sign. I never talked to anyone but my wife Terri about that night. For many years, I sometimes thought that it was my Grandpa talking through that older gentleman because it was so close to his house. I thought about it very hard for three weeks. I was not sure what to do. It was wintertime in 2002 and tons of commercials for the Army were on the air. It was right before the Iraq War was about to start. I was 24 years old at the time and was not doing anything with my life. I thought to myself, "If I ever want to be a part of a team again and travel the world right now, this is my opportunity." I went to the Army recruiter station in South County and enlisted around early December 2002. I did not tell anyone I would be in the delayed entry program for about four months.

I was pretty nervous, but very excited. I had a sense of purpose and was going to be a part of the most powerful team in the U.S. Army. I remember working out again like when I was playing basketball. I found my sense of purpose once again. It was a pretty crazy time watching commercials. The slogan then was *I am an Army of One.*

Around January 2003, my mom came over to visit me at my Aunt Mo's house. She brought something into my room and saw the army bag in my closet. I have always been a pretty quiet person and did not want people to worry about me, mainly because they could not do anything about it anyway. I have always been very stubborn and, once I make up my mind and commit to it, I would figure out some way to make it happen. Of course, my mom and dad, plus other family members, were scared for me and did not want me to go at first. That is why I did not tell anybody that I was going to enlist. I had to do this for me. If I told anybody about me enlisting, they might have tried to talk me out of it. Sometimes you just have to follow your heart and keep pushing forward.

The truth is your family and friends might have the best intentions for you, but you have to live your destiny. I would tell anybody to follow their dreams and go for it. Life can be short, and nobody knows when their time will be up in this world. I heard once that the richest place in the world is the graveyard, because there you find hopes and dreams that were never fulfilled. I decided I wanted to have the journey of a lifetime, and I knew I had to leave St. Louis to make it happen.

I remember thinking that one of the hardest things about leaving is not seeing my best friend, Terri. I met Terri at a very interesting place. I had a basketball game in Lakeland, IL, and I did not get home that Sunday until about midnight. I recall going over my buddy Scotty's house and meeting one of my best friend's brothers, Sal, there. We were just relaxing on the porch and decided to go to the nightclub Oz in East St. Louis. It was about 4:30 a.m. and the DJ played "I got the hook-up" by Master P. Man. You can't make this stuff up. That we the first song we danced too.

I remember seeing Terri for the first time and my world just froze. She was a beautiful, tall, young lady with a banging body. I had a few cocktails in me and asked her to dance. We enjoyed each other's company for about one hour. I got her number and called her up two days later. For about six years, Terri and I were best friends. She was the girl I always dreamed of but was never mature enough to have her give me a shot and take me seriously. I would not change anything though because we had some great conversations around 3 a.m. when all the pubs closed. We would always talk then, and it felt great to have a true friend to speak with.

It was about March 23, 2003, and we were celebrating at a bar called La Fayette, which is in Lafayette Park. I remember we were watching the TV up above, and it was showing the beginning of the Iraq War and all of the air strikes. Some guy overheard my buddies telling me good luck before I was supposed to start basic training March 26, 2003. I remember him telling me anyone who is about to go into the Army now is a loser with no other options. That pissed me off and I had a few choice words for him. I had so many emotions going on through my mind as I was leaving my family, Terri, all my friends, and the city. The guy pushed me, and I hit him a few times with a left and then my right. I hit him right in the forehead and felt my right knuckle just collapse. I now don't have a right knuckle—it collapsed. I felt like such a jackass. I went to the doctor the following day and had to get a brace on my fist for my finger that was broken.

On March 25, I had to go to the recruiter with a brace on my hand and explain to him what had happened. He was disappointed in me, and I was disappointed in myself. This incident could have easily been avoided if I had not gone out that night. It was 100% my fault; I let my family down and myself. The Army was attractive to me because I needed discipline in my life, especially after my basketball career had come to an end. Ever since I had stopped playing ball, I had lost that in my life and I was silently craving it.

My new date to start basic training was now June 26, 2003. Everything changed on this contract; the old one was void because they had to change where I was going to attend basic training. Originally, it was supposed to be at Fort Knox, Kentucky. I guess everything happens for a reason. Around June 25, 2006, my dad's best friend's daughter Mickey was getting married. I brought my best friend Terri to the wedding, even though I was seeing someone else. I remember it was at Windows on Washington and we had our first real kiss that night. I was leaving the next day and was focused on my new mission. I remember thinking to myself, "At least I got a real kiss from the girl I have always really cared about since we first met at the Oz six years ago."

The Decision to Serve: Embracing Duty Over Comfort

June 26, 2003 was the first day of basic training for me at Fort Jackson, South Carolina. I was 24 years old at that time which made me older than a lot of others at basic training. I had butterflies in my stomach when the plane touched down in South Carolina and the drill sergeants met us at night, yelling at us to get on the bus. We eventually got to Fort Jackson around midnight and they gave us a box of cereal and some juice. There were about 20 of us who slept on the floor at the barracks until the next morning at 0600.

My MOS was a 92G, which was a Food Service Specialist. I remember as a kid going to the Wetterau Bakery Warehouse where my dad worked. My dad worked very hard at the warehouse and always had a very strong work ethic. Around Halloween, my dad would always bring cupcakes home for me and my classmates. The cupcakes were great. Ever since I was a kid, my dad coached me and I wanted to be like him. I figured this would be a good military occupational specialty for me because I guessed it might be in my genes and I was a little familiar with it.

I remember meeting a guy named Eric Polgar from Indiana. He was a good guy and was close to my age. Basic training for me was a pretty good time. I was part of a team again, and that was something that I had really missed. I loved the camaraderie, doing obstacles and working together. One thing in the military is that if one person messes up, everyone pays the price. It teaches you to look out for your battle buddy and make sure they are squared away. They train us that way because when you are downrange in Iraq and Afghanistan, your buddies right by your side are all you have. They become your new family and you depend on one another.

Honestly, one of my favorite times about basic training was writing letters to Terri and getting mail. That is the only form of communication we had. You are totally cut off from the real world and have no idea what is going on. I think something happened while in basic—I was finally starting to grow up. I think Terri could tell that from my writing. I was not talking about where we were going to party Friday night; I was writing about things of substance, such as life. Even though we were hundreds of miles apart and were further away than we had ever been, through our writing, it seemed like we were getting closer than ever.

I completed basic training and then started Advanced Individual Training, or AIT, at Fort Lee, Virginia. We learned the basics and food preparation on the MKT (mobile kitchen trailer) and went out to the field for about one week. AIT was nine weeks long. After about four weeks, we got to make a phone call once a weekend when we went on pass. Terri and I started talking on the phone more and our relationship really started to heat up. While we were writing one another for about three months, we started to learn more about one another, and I started to fall in love even more with her. She started having the same feelings for me.

The last week before we graduated from AIT, the Drill Sergeants came out with our assignments and where we were going. "Smith, Timothy, you are going to Baumholder, Germany." I remember the two drill sergeants telling me, "Get ready to get hot because you are most likely going downrange. Baumholder, Germany, is primarily combat arms in the 1st armored division. They are deployed in Iraq right now," the drill sergeants explained to the three of us going to Baumholder, "I hope you paid attention in Basic Training because you are going to War!"

I called Terri and explained that I was going to be stationed in Baumholder, Germany. She got very quiet and stated she couldn't believe how far away we will be. I agreed with her and asked her to go to Las Vegas with me. I had two weeks on leave and the drill sergeants had a pretty good idea I was going to Iraq. I was lucky they drew my name to have an additional two weeks at home working with my recruiters. That would give me about 28 days to be with the love of my life, my dream girl: Terri.

It was nice to get back to St. Louis around the middle of November. Terri and I planned to go to Las Vegas about three days after I got home. Before I left for the Army, I weighed about 207 lbs and when I was out of basic training, I was a lean 178 lbs. Three square meals a day with no snacks in between, no alcohol, and a South Carolina 100-degree summer doing PT all day burned a lot of the extra fat.

Terri and I went to Las Vegas and I was planning to propose to her. We had a great time sightseeing and walking all along the Las Vegas strip. The night I proposed to Terri, we started out at about 7 p.m. at the Outback Steakhouse. The war in Iraq had just started around March 2003 and people seemed to be very supportive of the troops. Some guy recognized my haircut and figured out I was in the military and asked me what branch. I explained I was in the Army and getting ready to go to Baumholder, Germany. He gave me $20.00 and said to have a drink on him. I thought that was pretty awesome. I have been to Vegas a few times since and, when I talk to one service member, I always give them $20.00 to pay it forward. We met another older couple and they called themselves Ned and Ed the Winos. Ned, the female, was probably about 48 years old, and Ed was probably in his 50s. They bought us some drinks and Terri and I had dinner. I was not planning on having three cocktails, but people just bought them for us. About 11 p.m. at night, I proposed to Terri and got down on one knee in front of the gondola where the Venetian Hotel is located. She said yes! It was one of the happiest days of my life. I was going to marry the girl I had wanted to be with for over six years.

After hanging out another few weeks in St. Louis, I decided I did not want Terri to come over to Germany until I found out if I was going to get deployed or not. We both felt good about that decision because she would not know anyone and I was so new to the Regular Army. I had no idea what to expect.

3

Into the Fray: Baghdad and Brotherhood

Arrival in Iraq: Stepping Into the Unknown

When I first arrived at Baumholder, Germany around December 2003, I received my assignment. I was being assigned to the 1st Armored Division 4-27FA. The unit I was being assigned to had already been in Iraq for about seven months and 15 of us were going downrange as replacements because the violence was gearing up. The guy I call a brother now, I met him the second day when I got to Baumholder. His name is Carlos Cardenas from South Central, LA . Carlos is about 6'3" and a big guy who was a 13B which is a Field Artillery gunner. Out of the 15 of us, 13 guys were 13B, while two of us were combat support

We were in Baumholder when we got the news that a medic Doc Hollis who was in 4-27 was killed in action (KIA). The 15 of us were detailed to receive his body at Ramstein Air Force base. After that day, everything became very real to us—all of us were fresh out of basic training and AIT. The next week, we trained at a post in Germany for three days, and the following week, we were catching up with our unit in Baghdad, Iraq. We all got really drunk that night and started singing the Red Hot Chili Peppers song "Under the Bridge" because we knew shit was about to get real!

We arrived in Baghdad around January 6. When our plane touched down at the Baghdad International Airport (BIAP), it was pouring down rain. I could not believe that. I thought to myself, "This is Iraq; I never knew it rained here. Later on, we were brought to a tent where about 30 of us stayed. We were going to have two days of training before we were issued our weapon and go catch up with our unit 4-27FA, who was at the Thunder FOB (Forward Operating Base) in the heart of downtown Baghdad.

The second night we were at BIAP, we took about five mortar rounds.

I remember listening to Evanescence with my headphones and feeling the ground shake. About five mortars hit pretty close to us and you could see in the ground where they hit. A few of the guys who were in the country for a while kind of laughed at us. They asked where we were going and told us to have fun. They knew we were going to a much smaller FOB that was right in the middle of the city. Carlos and I kind of looked at each other like, "What the hell are we getting ourselves into?"

We were issued our weapons at BIAP and the rest of the time, my weapon was with me. We were all issued the M16A2 and seven magazines of 30 rounds each – a basic combat load. I remember we were picked up in a 2½-ton vehicle. It was about 2100 hours, which in civilian time is 9 p.m. When we first left the base, it was nighttime. We got on the highway, and there was a convoy of five vehicles. We were about 45 minutes away from our new home. I remember the first time driving in the back of our Deuce and a Half, with our weapons pointed outwards. I was about one month out of Basic Training and AIT in the Regular Army, and my first duty station was Baghdad, Iraq. There were tons of people on the streets, just walking around. We saw a few stores in the city that were lit up with lights. My heart was pounding and there was an adrenaline rush. It was still hard for me to believe that I was downrange now and that it was real.

Daily Battles: Facing the Physical and Emotional Demands of War

When I first got to Thunder FOB in Baghdad, it was a learning experience. My unit had already been there for about eight months. We were the newbies, and it takes some time to earn the respect of everyone else. When the 15 of us replacements got there, we were definitely at the bottom of the barrel and rightfully so. Our unit had already been there for eight months, working 16-18 hours daily with no days off.

They had KBR (Kellogg, Brown, and Root) all over Iraq that made the meals for all of the soldiers so we would not do our regular military operational service. Our NCOs were very squared away and showed us the ropes very fast. They were tough on us, but for a very good reason. One of the jobs we would do is go to the green zone every morning about 0430 to pick up the chow. Our FOB was about 35 minutes away in the red zone. We had four vehicles in our convoy every morning that consisted of two Humvees and two 5-tons. We had four different routes that we would switch up every morning. At that time in the morning, it was still pretty dark outside. Every morning, we would check our comms (communication) in the Humvees and 5-tons to make sure everyone was on the same channel. We would put the pedal to the metal and ride centered in the middle of the street, because on the sides of the street was where the terrorists would hide all of the Improvised Explosive Devices (IEDs).

We would pick up the chow from KBR around 0545 and then load it up in the 5-tons, and then we would go back to thunder FOB. Around 0615, when we would be bringing the chow back home, the sunrise would come. The sunrise was very beautiful and I can still see it in my mind. It was always very orange and red, almost like a burning red. Every morning, we heard their prayers going throughout their loudspeakers all over the city. This would happen five times a day. The first time I heard it, I was like, "What in the hell is that?" They told me and laughed and said get ready for it. We would then leave the FOB at 1530 and bring back the mermites. We would then get dinner from KBR and bring it back to our FOB around 1700 hours. We would get done serving the chow at about 1900 hours, then clean up until about 2000 hours. You get in a routine of doing that day in and day out, with no days off.

Another duty I did a lot of was guard duty. We would do 12-hour shifts around Thunder FOB. We had a brick wall that surrounded us that was about 15 feet tall and there were eight guard posts that were about 20 feet tall. Our job was to look for BOLO (Be On the LookOut) vehicles and then report them to headquarters. Every two hours, we would relieve each other and then move to the next tower. We were right in the middle of a Baghdad neighborhood, so we always had to keep a close lookout. There were always gunshots being heard throughout the city and explosions. The rooms that we would sleep in were pretty close to the walls. Some of the terrorists would throw grenades right over the walls and would launch mortars at our building.

That is why every two hours we would relieve another soldier in front of us—to stay alert. We never really kept track of the days, because it did not matter. There were no weekends, and all of the days ran together. We were lucky and had a basketball court right by the makeshift chow hall. In our down time, we got to play basketball and that was pretty cool. I was able to meet some very good guys playing ball just like when I was a child. It made me think of my family and friends back home.

We went to the range a few times and we would fire our weapons and train up on them. I started firing the 50 caliber a lot and got very used to it. The ranges were nothing but desert and some targets. All of our artillery was in the motor pool at our FOB in Baghdad. All of our unit was pretty much trying to gather information in the cities and doing patrols. Out there, our unit was able to fire the artillery. My eyes started swelling up and I looked like I had two pieces of pepperoni on my eyes from firing so many 50 cal rounds. I could hardly see; my eyes were very irritated and the skin looked cracked below them. I would see my buddy Doc Darling and he would give me some Benadryl and then I would put warm washcloths under my eyes. I was able to perform my duties every day, but Doc and I got pretty close because he would hook me up with the Benadryl. Doc Darling was 29 years old and always had a smile on his face. He was always drinking protein shakes and trying to work out when he was not on shift. He was a morale booster and always brought a smile to other soldiers' faces.

4

Sacrifice and Remembrance

Brothers in Arms: Unbreakable Bonds and Lasting Friendships

It was April 2004—and things in Baghdad were starting to heat up. Iraq was getting ready to have its first elections since Saddam was overthrown. Some of the Iraqis were happy about this and others were very pissed off about it. Every morning before we left the FOB, we would get the report if the roads were green, red, or black. The roads were black for about three weeks with people protesting in the streets everywhere. At times, in the city, we would have to get out of our vehicles to make a pathway. We did not have any armored vehicles at that time and would put sandbags in our Humvees and five tons; in case we hit an IED, it would take some of the impact. Our mechanics were squared away and would find some scrap armor and weld it on our vehicles for makeshift armor. We could feel the city of Baghdad heating up, and we would have to watch our backs. There were a lot of tall buildings where snipers would post up at and on the ground, and there were IEDs everywhere. The city of Baghdad was going up in flames. Thunder FOB started taking many more mortar rounds and IEDs. One of the mechanics whom I first roomed with was walking around the FOB, and he looked down at his wrist when a bullet went straight through it. Sometimes I don't know if Iraqis knew what goes up must come down.

There was talk about an extension around April 2004. I felt bad because the guys in my unit had already been there a year. I was lucky I had only been in the county for about three and a half months. The word came down from Lt. Col McKiernan and he explained we would be getting extended another three months and the stop-loss went into effect (stop-loss meant no one could leave). A few guys from our unit were supposed to be leaving pretty soon, but that was not going to happen. Everyone was staying in Iraq, and we had another important mission. We would be leaving Thunder FOB and moving to a new location. None of us knew where that was going to be. About two weeks before the extension, 1st Cav was coming to replace us at Thunder FOB while we waited to get to get our orders and push into a different FOB.

One of the last nights before 1st Cav was getting ready to do "left seat right seat" with our unit, we celebrated our extension. We had casual day at our FOB a few days before we got the news. The most you could take out from the ATM was $200 and a lot of us did. The only thing to spend money on was the $2 Haji movies and some knockoff Red Bull drink called Wild Tiger. We were all sitting flush with cash, but nothing to spend it on. We started a huge craps game, starting off with people betting $10 a roll and eventually it got up to $75 a roll. We were like young boys again, just laughing about things that made no sense. There were about 14 of us in a room that was probably 50' x 30'. We drove each other nuts, but at the end of the day, we had each other's back. You get to know everything about one another in a very short amount of time. Everybody had a nickname—my name was either Smitty or Smitty Rock because I was always rocking back and forth. I guess I got that from my mom because she does the same thing. I will always remember that night. Everybody was singing or rapping, walking around with their Promask on and just was carefree that night. A few days later, 1st Cav relived us and took over our living quarters.

In the last week and a half, we all slept on cots in the motor pool outside by our vehicles while we trained 1st Cav on the routes we used and what we were doing. We started taking a lot more mortar fire and the streets got more dangerous. The Iraqis are fierce fighters that have been fighting for thousands of years. They knew a different unit was taking over the area of Baghdad that our unit patrolled and wanted to capitalize on a new unit taking over the territory. The guys from 1st Cav seemed squared away for the two weeks we worked besides them.

We got our orders and, at first, we were going to FOB Striker at BIAP and then some of us would be going to Al-Mahmud Iyah, taking over FOB St. Michael. The Marines were pushing into Fallujah. It was going to be a different environment for us; Baghdad was very urban with many tall buildings and Mahmudiyah was going to be very rural. Our unit was finally going to be firing our artillery and doing what we were trained to do.

At this time, I was only a PFC and only knew limited intel. We would do our job to the best of our ability and look out after one another.

We went in different chalks and were able to get all of our vehicles to FOB Striker at BIAP. It was a pretty tense time, and the battle of Fallujah was just starting. Iraq was filled with IEDs on the ground—with daisy chains where they would connect two or three explosive devices that could really hurt a convoy. We were used to items such as vehicles burning on the sides of the roads, and the air was always black there. It was like LA on steroids, with the pollution up above.

We all got to FOB Striker and it was pretty nice. There was tons of space, and we had about 30 soldiers to a tent. We had telephones that were about a half mile away, which accepted phone cards, and I would call Terri. I missed her so much; we were supposed to get married in April, but, of course, that was pushed back. We would do preventive maintenance check and services (PMCS) of our vehicles a lot and do log packs while we were there, basically picking up supplies from other FOBs and other duties.

The Cost of Freedom: Loss, Honor, and the Price Paid

Around April 28, 2004, we were going to the PX at BIAP. About 30 of us were getting ready to go to FOB St. Michael in Mahmudiyah. We were grabbing items like toothpaste, sports drinks, and CDs to listen to because we would not have access to items like this anymore about a week later. We even had some chow at the only Burger King in Iraq at the time.

I remember talking with my buddy Doc Darling about his two girls and how he could not wait to talk with them. His eyes would light up as he spoke about them on our way back to FOB Striker. We stopped by a small Haji market on the side of the road. Doc Darling was very excited because he was able to buy one of those minute phones to call his daughters.

On April 29, 2004, I remember walking back to the tent because I was just getting off guard duty. My buddy Carlos called me over and said, "Timmy, did you hear what happened?" Carlos is like my brother; we met the second night in Germany and always were very close. He said that eight of our brothers were killed in action by a remote detonated car bomb while doing a patrol. He said that Norman (Doc) Darling was one of them. I could not believe it; I was just with him yesterday and he was buying a phone to talk to his little girls. I was numb, like many of the other soldiers in my unit. We did not talk about our feelings because it would have been too painful. I just walked by myself and cried. These guys were all so young and paid the ultimate sacrifice. Their names were Staff Sergeant Esau Patterson Jr., Staff Sergeant Jeffrey Dayton, Sgt. Ryan Campbell, Spc James Beckstrand, Spc Justin Schmidt, PFC Ryan Reed, PFC Norman (Doc) Darling, and PVT Jeremy Ewing.

A few days later, they had a memorial for them at FOB Striker. That was the hardest memorial I had ever attended. They had eight pairs of boots with their weapons and Kevlar, with their names on them. They had a few soldiers talk about each one of them and things they really cared about. Towards the end, the CSM called each of their names while doing the last roll call. It was very quiet and almost no one was looking up. I knew I was not. The last song before it ended was "American Solider" by Toby Keith. Whenever I hear that song, it brings me back to that day and all of the feelings associated with it.

A few days after the memorial, about 20 of us were getting ready to go to FOB St. Michael in Mahmudiyah. They called it the Triangle of Death because it was right by Fallujah and Yusuphia. There was very intense fighting at that time because the Battle of Fallujah was going on. They transported us using two 5-tons, and we all piled up in there like sardines. We had a few guns providing security for us on the ride there. The roads on the way there were different than the ones we were used to. It was a lot of dirt roads and open space. There were not any tall buildings we had to scan anymore; now it was looking at dead animals on the sides of the road. The Iraqis would put IEDs anywhere they thought could kill troops. We still did not have any up armor and almost all the vehicles were softshell.

The Marines pushed into Fallujah a few weeks prior, the 1st Armored Division took over FOB St. Michael. It was different units from Baumholder, Germany, working together. Our unit brought in the Paladins and was providing outgoing fire. When we first arrived at the FOB, in huge letters it said, "STAY ALERT, STAY ALIVE." There were many Hesco Barriers all over the FOB to help protect from mortar rounds and RPG Fire. The FOB was pretty small and was surrounded with Concertina wire. We slept on bunk beds—about 20 guys. Our housing unit was made out of thin plywood, and then there were sandbags on top to take some of the mortar rounds' impact.

I got my assignment to Tower 5, which was right by a little creek from which you could see a small house about 800 meters out and then a bunch of palm trees about 1200 meters back. My battle buddy's name was Simpson, a really cool black surfer from California. He was a very spiritual guy and a hell of a soldier. He was very muscular and was always talking about what he could not wait to eat when he went home. The shifts we would pull there were six hours on and then six hours off. Our tower was right over the Concertina wire and we would joke around and say if our tower ever did get hit, we were going to be tangled up all in the Concertina wire. We were used to taking mortar rounds and RPG fire at Thunder FOB, but FOB St. Michael was much smaller.

On our second shift, there were about six mortar rounds that fell right around us. We had the saw gun upon our tower, and I grabbed that right away. Simpson used the comms to talk and see what area we were taking fire from. It was very difficult for us to see where we were taking fire from because of the palm tree covers, and a lot of times, they would ride up in their white pickup trucks with part of it being orange and then take off. I can still see the dirt just flying into the air from the impact rounds coming in all around us.

About three minutes after that, we heard over the comms "Outgoing fire," then we heard the Paladins firing. The Paladins were about 30 meters away from us and made the tower shake when they fired the rounds. We would see a fireball coming from the cannons and our ears would ring quite a bit, because of the thunderous boom. We were supposed to wear ear plugs but most of us did not. We had to listen to the incoming fire and try to locate the area it was coming from.

About three weeks later, we were used to all of their incoming mortar rounds and RPGs. One thing I used to hate about the incoming RPGs is that you could hear the whistle and then about three seconds later, it would hit and blow up loudly as hell. For those three seconds though, you would kind of hold your breath because you had no idea where it was going to hit. I remember one day, about an hour after Simpson and I got off guard duty, we went back to our sleeping quarters. I think it was about 1630 hours, because people were getting ready to go to chow. We heard a few RPGs whizzing towards us, followed by some mortar rounds. We were pretty used to this by now.

This time though, they just kept falling on us. Most of the time, it lasted only about a minute. This time, they were walking the mortar rounds in on us and you could feel the earth shaking with each round falling. One soldier ran into our sleeping quarters to take cover because we had sandbags above us to take some of the impact. He yelled, "People are getting fucked up everywhere." I looked in his eyes and could see the fear. This attack probably lasted about seven minutes, which does not seem like a long time, but when mortar rounds are falling about ten meters away from you, it seems like an eternity. Luckily, our sleeping quarters and our battle buddies right next to us were not hit. About 22 soldiers were wounded that day, but we were very lucky because there was no one killed in action. The 2-6 Infantry and 1-35 Armor were also at FOB St. Michael, working hand and hand with us. 4-27FA was lucky that day not to have any injuries. 2-6 Inf and 1-35 Armor were about 35 meters and all their rows of tents are the ones that got hit very hard that day.

The next month, we took a lot of incoming and tons of outgoing fire. At night, you could see star clusters which would light up the sky. We would see these all through the night. Simpson and I would have some deep conversations, because you get to know each other very well when you are with one another 24/7.

I would talk to him about how I could not wait to marry Terri and how we met. He would have a few laughs and explained to me that I am a lucky man. Simpson was from California and grew up around a lot of Hispanics and was very familiar with the culture. Sometimes, I think back to those conversations because they were so honest, and we did not know if we were going to live or die the next day.

There was always black smoke in the air from the burn pits. All of us were sucking in that pollution every day. You don't think about it at the time; you just do what you have to do. Sometimes, after guard duty, we would have to do other jobs around the FOB. A few times, we would go to the weapons cache, which was full of smaller rockets and mortar rounds. We would line up and pass the explosives to set them in a 5-ton where some guys would pick them up and then do a controlled explosion with them. This was about the end of June, and it was about 130 degrees outside every day. It was kind of freaky handling these explosives because it was so hot that sometimes, they would start smoking. Nothing ever blew up on us; I am very thankful for that.

We finished our time there and we were getting ready to go back to Baumholder, Germany. Everybody was extremely excited and could not wait to get back home. Our unit had been there for 15 months, but I was very lucky and was only there for 6½ months. Around July 13, 2004, some of us touched down in Baumholder, Germany. We had to do a seven-day reintegration back in Baumholder where they asked us many questions. If you answered them a certain way, you would not be able to go on 30-day block leave when you got home. I don't know anyone then who answered the questions and said they were having some difficulties. Everyone just wanted to get home to their loved ones. I could not believe I was going home to marry the love of my life. I was ready to go back home to St. Louis. I still remember getting off the plane in St. Louis and seeing Terri for the first time in about 7½ months. I just looked at her and gave her a huge hug and kiss. It felt so good to hold her in my arms again. I was reunited with my best friend and soon-to-be wife in two days. My mom, dad, Aunt Mo, and sister were there also. It was so good to see everyone's face.

Terri and I talked, and we planned to get married at the St. Louis County Court house. I was married in my Class A's and Terri had a beautiful dress. I kind of feel bad because I could not afford to give her the perfect wedding in a church with the white dress she wanted. I was a PFC in the Army and even though I had saved up my combat pay, I could not afford to have a big wedding. Honestly, I just wanted to be with her anyways and just had a few close family and friends get together. We had a little reception at McGurk's down in Soulard and that was great. After that, Terri and I spent the night at a beautiful hotel in the Central West End, the Chase Park Plaza. For our honeymoon, Terri and I visited California. She had a lot of family that lives there, plus my battle buddy Carlos lives there. We went to Disneyland and had a great time. It was my first time ever at Disneyland and I felt like a kid again. I remember when I was a kid, my parents took my sister and me to Disney World. It brought back a lot of memories of being a kid when life was much simpler. I remember thinking to myself, "Just three weeks ago, I was in Iraq, ducking and dodging mortar rounds, and now I am in 'It's a Small World After All.'" It's a pretty different environment than the one I had just experienced.

5

Coming Home: A Different Kind of War

Home Yet Not Home: The Challenges of Transition

About 30 days later, Terri was able to come over to Germany with me as a dependent and we were able to get housing one mile off post at Champion Village. It was a nice little two-bedroom apartment that was just ours and we had a great time together. I was 25 and Terri was 24 years old. It was like a honeymoon in Germany when I was not in field training.

Six months after we got married, Terri and I found out we were pregnant. We were excited and nervous because this was the first time we were going to be parents. This was a new chapter in our lives. I felt alive again. I was going to be a dad and be able to do all the things my parents did for me. I was thrilled.

At the time, Baumholder was having a baby boom because we all got back from deployment at the same time and had some catching up to do with our wives. We had to go to a German doctor off post, in a little town by Birkenfeld. A lot of the military spouses and soldiers had to go to these doctors because Baumholder did not have the capacity for this many births at the same time. About five months into Terri's pregnancy, we found out we were having a little boy. I was going to have a little boy!

Terri's Mom Ana came to visit Germany and stay with us for a few months since we were going to have our first child. I remember how nervous I was when Terri was in labor. There was nothing I could do besides hold her hand and support her. On October 24, 2005, we were blessed with a beautiful baby boy. When Timmy was born, he was born with a port wine stain on the left side of his cheek and above his left eye. I called it his warrior mark because he was born around soldiers and I knew he would be a warrior and a leader. I remember changing his first diaper about half an hour after he was born and promising him I would always be there for him and teach him everything he would need to know to be a great kid and then man. I was so proud to be his dad and to share the rest of my life with my best friend Terri and Little man, Timmy Jr.

Since I was in a Field Artillery unit, we would go to Grafenwöhr and Hohenfels often to train for about 30-45-day field exercises. It was really nice that Terri's mom stayed with her because I was in the field training a lot. I was training as part of a PSD (Personal Security Detail) team for the CSM and LTC and would get called at all different times of the day and night because, whenever they called, we would train and pull security for them. I remember the way to Grafenwöhr, my buddy Big Karl Eason and I driving together on which was about a nine-hour convoy with a bunch of Humvees and 5-tons. It was a very long drive, but we had a lot of time to talk and get to know each other. Eason was from Texas and was a hell of a nice guy. He would take his shirt off his back and give it to you. We trained and Big Karl was our 50 cal gunner and I was a driver. The PSD team consisted of many different MOS/military occupational specialties working together. We were training and our unit was getting ready to redeploy back to Iraq in about four months. My eyes started to swell again while I was in the field. Those big red bags that were swollen reappeared and, at times, it was difficult for me to see and it was frustrating. I felt like I was letting my team down and, internally, I struggled with it. I was a soldier and was able to get through the swollen eye issues while downrange, and now it was starting again.

The Weight of the Past: Confronting Invisible Wounds

About a month and a half before I was to redeploy again, I found out I was stay on rear-detachment because of the issues I was having with my eyes. At the time, I was E-4 promotable and was going to make SGT pretty soon. I remember my E-6 coming to tell me, "Smitty," at the D-Fac (Dining Facility), "we need one soldier to stay back to take care of the ration room." I felt many emotions when he gave me the news. I felt like I was letting down my unit and my team. I have been training with them and had experience downrange. On the other hand, I was kind of relieved because I experienced firsthand all the emotions felt by soldiers in a combat zone and could still visualize in my mind some of the crazy things we experienced.

My son Timmy Jr. was three months old at the time. Service members have to leave their children all the time for deployments; that has to be one of the hardest things in the world. I felt very fortunate, but I struggled everyday, quietly feeling like a failure and letting them down.

Back in the rear, I worked in the rations room. I would do all the ordering of the different food items, take inventory, and balance the book so that everything matched up with AFMIS (Army Food Management Information System). At this time, we had German contractors preparing all of the chow. Baumholder was always deploying, so the Army contracted out all of the actual cooking. For me, honestly that was a very good thing. I was not a good cook and, while in the service, had only prepared a few meals. I have to say though, I was really enjoying the ration room, and it made me think about accountability and how it was huge in the Army. If everything did not match up, there were going to be questions that needed to be answered. Some of my responsibilities included doing inspections in the DFAC and doing quality management checks on cleanliness. I had a checklist and had to make sure that everything was disinfected and cleaned. I would have to top scrub some of the DFAC's floor and we had GI cleaning parties where everything would be cleaned from top to bottom. I always enjoyed seeing the facility before and after pictures because you could see the difference between the two pics and feel a sense of accomplishment.

At the same time I was working, Terri and Timmy Jr and I were a family, and I felt so lucky to be able to spend time with them. We took Timmy Jr. to a few of the Army doctors and they explained that a laser treatment could help his blood flow circulation and the port wine stain could get lighter over time. Like any parent, I wanted the best for him and wanted him to be healthy. Back in St. Louis, Missouri, they have a children's hospital that specializes in port wine stain laser treatments. Terri took a military hop and was able to take him to St. Louis for his first time for the procedure. I stayed back in Germany and worked. I was happy because he was going to be seen by the medical professionals who could provide us with good information.

In early 2006, I earned Sergeant stripes, so of course that was more responsibility. I worked in the ration room for six months and gained some really good experience that could help me in the civilian world. I knew I was going to have to leave the Army because my eyes were jacked up, but I would have to do something to support my family. A position opened up for the Administration (NCO) and I said I would like to be trained up. This experience made me a lot more familiar with computers and technology. This was one of my weak spots, and I was intimidated by computers. I only had 15 hours left to graduate college, but I was able to type those up and then turn it into my professors. I really did not email that much and did not have much confidence in myself when it came to that. Working in Admin NCO, I would have to email, collect money, estimate how many people will come to chow, enter information into the computer, and do the books so that all the emails and cash by civilian contractors added up.

Over time, I really enjoyed the admin side of work and felt comfortable working with numbers and estimating the number of soldiers and civilians that would come to the chow hall on certain days of the week. During this time, I was around soldiers that were downrange before and I was still a part of a team. Like I said earlier, I was always used to being a part of a team and having some mission to concentrate on that I was a part of. And in the military, you stay very busy and time flies by fast.

At night, I would wake up sometimes if I thought I heard something and would sit up very fast. My heart rate would rise, and I would start sweating. My wife Terri would always ask if I was okay. I would get some water and sit up for about ten minutes. I was having dreams about being downrange and I could still see the mortar rounds falling all around me and hear the outgoing artillery. I never really talked about that while I was in Germany—none of us did. At the time, I was a SGT and had a few soldiers underneath me. I wanted to make sure to keep it to myself because I did not want it to affect my rank.

I had about four months left in the Army and I was going to ETS (Expiration Term of Service). Our unit had about two weeks left being downrange and they were getting ready to come back to Baumholder.

Everyone was very happy they were coming back to Baumholder. I received a phone call and was told to report to Battalion. They called us and said that SPC Karl Eason was killed In Action. My heart fell to the ground again and I was numb. I felt horrible because I trained with him and was his driver. I felt and still feel a lot of guilt. I don't know if anything would have been different had I been there with him, but you always ask yourself that question. I was there in 2004 and I was fighting in Iraq. I went to his memorial on post in Baumholder and paid my respects. I felt privileged to serve with a real hero that paid the ultimate sacrifice. The world lost another great guy and his two girls lost their dad. Being a father now, I could only imagine how hard that is on the kids and I would pray for them. It was great to see my battle buddies get home and reunite with their families. Everybody was getting ready to ETS or PCS (go to another duty station). I learned many things from my four years in the Army, such as how to adapt, work long hours, discipline, and face challenges head-on. And how to be a part of a family and something much bigger than yourself.

I was Honorably Discharged from the Army on February 16, 2007. I had no idea what I wanted to do with my life and was nervous because I was leaving the Army, wondering how I would support my wife and son. I noticed the closer it got to the date I left the Army, the more nervous I got. When you are in the Army, you are surrounded by soldiers 24/7 and you are never alone. You have that sense of security. Before you ETS, you start feeling more alone with not as many soldiers who are around you. I started struggling with nightmares more often, waking up startled, and looking for my weapon. I was ending my military career and never addressed some issues I should have. If I stayed busy, my goal was not to think about any of the issues that I was facing.

6

New Beginnings: From Soldier to Scholar

The Mission Continues: A Path to Purpose and Community

On February 16, 2007, I was Honorably Discharged from the Regular Army. Terri, Timmy Jr., and I moved back to St. Louis and were fortunate to move in with my Aunt Mo. She has always been like my second mom. We were living with her in South St. Louis off Arsenal Street. Aunt Mo lived right by a fire station, so we would hear the sirens at night. Timmy Jr loved walking by the fire house and looking in. I tried every day for six months to find a job and was getting turned down day after day. I did not have my bachelor's in social work yet and for a good number of jobs, you needed the diploma. I started to apply for labor jobs or any job that would help me support my family. I was going to school at that time, so my GI bill would give me about $1,300 a month that would help support us while I was going to school.

The first six months were the hardest for me to transition. I was diagnosed with PTSD, severe chronic conjunctivitis in my eyes, and tinnitus in my ears from all the outgoing artillery while in Iraq. I was having difficulties sleeping and I would isolate myself. I did not like big crowds because it reminded me of the city of Baghdad, being surrounded by people, never knowing what to expect. I would wake up at night searching for my weapon if I heard something loud. While deployed, you have your weapon 24/7 and it is like a security blanket for a small child. You feel safe with it.

One morning, while attending class at UMSL, I was walking through the hallway that was all windows and you could see the lights shining very brightly and it almost blinded me for a minute. I saw a Muslim man dressed in traditional clothing and broke out in a sweat. There was a restroom about 10 feet away where I rinsed my face off with water to snap back to reality.

I was feeling faint and seeing stars, like when you have trouble breathing. The bright sunlight and seeing the traditional wear the man was wearing brought me back to that place and some of the emotions I experienced over there. Also, I felt a sense of guilt. I would ask myself sometimes how I was so lucky not to get hit by a mortar round, RPG, or hit an IED while driving. Maybe a lot of veterans feel that sometimes; it is a feeling that stays with you all the time. I started going to counseling at the VA and that helped me very much. I worked with Dr. Mastnak and she normalized some of the feelings I was having. Every week, my symptoms started to decrease a little. I was learning different strategies to deal with the pain and how to set short term goals to get me through each week.

I was finally able to find work and I was hired at the main post office downtown. I was called a part-time regular and I was a mail handler. My hours were from midnight to 6 a.m., Wednesday through Sunday. I was stoked to get a job and finally start working again. I felt like I was able to support my family again instead of just looking for work. I worked on low cost four upstairs and would separate all the mails by different zip codes. After I got off work, I would go to school from 8 a.m. to noon. I was busy, but I thought about a lot of things and this helped me out. I was around a good number of veterans while working at the post office and that was a good thing. I was not isolating myself as much and was able to connect with others who had been through some of the same experiences.

Washington University: A Second Chance at Education

When I was going through counseling at the VA PTSD clinic, they found out my goal was to be a social worker. The head of psychology at the time suggested that I would try to get into the Brown School of Social Work at Washington University in St. Louis. I grew up in St. Louis my whole life and never even thought about going to a school like that. That was where all the kids that had money and were smart went. I definitely did not have that kind of money and made average grades. My parents were excited when I got a full ride for basketball at Forest Park Community College and were ecstatic when I received my bachelor's from UMSL. Going to grad school never really crossed my mind. Dr. Gaioni asked me to meet with Dr. Monica Mathieu, who at the time worked for the Brown School of Social Work. I was kind of laughing to myself, thinking this was a waste of time; however, I thought to myself, "I have nothing to lose."

So I went to apply at the Brown School and met with Monica. I recall walking up to Monica's office to meet with her. I was intimidated at first because, in my mind, it still seemed impossible to get into the #1 school of social work in the U.S. When I met with Monica, I felt at home. She walked me through the application process and we talked about my life experience; that is one thing that Brown looks for. I talked about my time going down to the Boys Club in St. Louis and how that had a big impact on me wanting to help out my community. I also talked about my time in the military and how we worked with every race, ethnicity, social economic status, and gender to come together as a team to accomplish a mission.

I was 29 years old at the time and had more life experience than the other students who were 23 and 24 years old. I worked on the application packet for two weeks. Monica was kind enough to proofread my application. My grammar was weak, and I saw a lot of red marks. I needed to work on that, but at least she proofread my work and I was able to make the changes before I turned in the packet. The packet consisted of five questions and I wrote about ten pages. It was a lot of work to just apply. I was happy just to turn in the packet.

A month later, a letter came to my Aunt Mo's house. It was an acceptance letter. I got into the Brown School of Social Work at Washington University in St. Louis. I was a Service-Connected Disabled Veteran so VA Voc Rehab would pay my full tuition and purchase my books. That acceptance letter changed my life because I would be exposed to a world I knew nothing about. I was still working nights at the main post office downtown so I would bring note cards and study different social work theories while on break and when we were slow at work. The guys at work would ask, "Tim, what the hell are you looking at?"

I told them I had to catch up on studying because I was starting a MSW program and had to catch up with all the other students. I had about seven months before I would start grad school and I was preparing for school working with Monica. Monica told me about this guy Eric Greitens who was a Navy Seal and Rhodes Scholar and wanted to help other veterans who served. I got off the night shift at 6 a.m. and went home, showered up, and went to meet Eric at his office at 8 a.m. The first person I met was Rachel Wald, a very nice and intelligent lady that obtained her undergrad at Duke. She told me to have a seat on Eric's couch and that he would be into talk to me in about five minutes. While sitting on the couch, I was nervous; I was going to be speaking to an officer. When Eric first came in, he smiled and introduced himself. I said, "Nice to meet you, sir," pretty quietly. Over the next hour and a half, Eric and I hit it off and I felt very comfortable talking to him. We talked about our time in the service, where we were stationed at downrange in Iraq, and what I wanted to do now to serve my country again.

I talked to Eric about how I used to go to the Boys Club of St. Louis in Soulard from when I was about 8 to 16 years old and how that place gave me a solid foundation of what it means to be a part of a community giving back. I also talked to him about how my dream was working with other veterans and being a part of a team again. I explained to him how my dream was to work at the VA. I just did not know how I was going to do that. Eric talked to me about his dream, The Mission Continues, which was first called Center for Citizen Leadership. This is where I could do my fellowship at the VA.

Honestly, at first, I was not sure what a fellowship was, but it sounded like a great opportunity to work with other veterans. Eric and I drove to the Boys Club of St. Louis and the VA to look into a fellowship working as a peer support counselor, where I would help my fellow veterans that went through similar situations I did and provide information to them while also providing peer support. This was my dream job, and I was so excited. I would do The Mission Continues Fellowship from 7:30 a.m. to 3 p.m., while working nights at the post office from midnight to 6 a.m. The fellowship paid about $1,000 a month, a stipend which would help me support my family. Just five months before, I felt low and ashamed of myself for going to the state and applying for food stamps. Life at that time was very difficult for me and I was very low. The first 11 months before I started my fellowship were the lowest in my life I had ever been. The first six months were the toughest because I was not going to school or working. The time would pass so slowly and all I had was time to think about the past and things that I could not change. I felt a lot of guilt and was ashamed, second-guessing myself, saying if I would have done this instead, maybe that mortar would have not landed on my buddy and different scenarios like that. Over time and with counseling, my psychologist normalized those situations for me and I started to forgive myself and started to see the future, and it looked so much brighter. For me, personally, the busier I became, the lesser my symptoms of PTSD affected me. Of course, those thoughts are always there, but the busier I stayed and the clearer I made my goals, the more doors started to open.

I started doing my fellowship at the VA as a peer support counselor and also started getting the word out about The Mission Continues. At that time, The Mission Continues consisted of Eric Greitens, Rachel Wald, and me in St. Louis, Missouri. I would go to different events, setting up The Mission Continues tent and passing out information. I would call different organizations like the St. Louis Science Center, Boys Club, and Girls Club of St. Louis, Missouri, and Humane Society and try to form partnerships for other fellows. At that time, a lot of people had not heard of The Mission Continues and were not sure about the organization. I learned how to make cold calls and talk to people to try to get the word out. At first, a lot of people thought we were too young of an organization and did not want to work with us. I learned a lot about how to deal with rejection and to not take it personally. I knew The Mission Continues could help out many veterans because it was helping me out.

Each day, I felt more confidence in myself and I just thought to myself, "What if I could be a part of something like The Mission Continues?" I was 100% on board. I learned how to set short-term goals that would eventually get me to my long-term goals. I learned from Eric about how there are green lights and red lights. You are going to be able to accomplish your goals or you will not. There really is no middle. It's great that you try, but at the end of the day, you have to measure your goals and make sure you are accomplishing them. In my life now, as a business owner, I win bids to hire veterans and feed my family or I do not and we lose the bid. I don't get points for trying, I get paid to produce cleaning results every day. I love the challenge and the pressure and lessons like those have paid off greatly.

When I was about four to nine years old, I remember writing about my speech impediment. Part of my fellowship at The Mission Continues was publicly speaking about my experience in the military and how I wanted to help out the veteran community. I was about two months into my fellowship. Paul Eisenstein, who had just gotten hired on about two weeks prior, was driving Eric and me. Paul is one of the nicest guys I have ever met and was passionate about helping veterans. That being said, Paul and I were both really green at these events. Eric was even newer to going to these events, but he did not show it. We were going to the Ladue Golf Country Club where Eric would talk about his experience as a Navy Seal and then I would talk about my experience. As a Mission Continues fellow, this was very intimidating for me to do at first. I would think to myself, "What I am I doing in this room, talking to these people who grew up very differently than I did?"

I remember going to the bathroom before I spoke and just making sure that my suit was squared away. I spoke for about seven minutes that evening and did a pretty good job. All the members were very nice, and I had a great time sitting with the members at my table. I was listening to private business owners and they were talking about their assets and liabilities. I had never really listened to conversations like those ones and they piqued my interest. All of these ladies and men were talking about winning contracts, and then they would find team members and pay them an hourly wage. It was a life-changing experience, and I realized I was judging them a lot more than they were judging me. After that day, I changed my perceptions on how I felt about people who had money. They wanted to share information with a guy like me. Before attending that event, I had told myself silently that I don't belong in a room with these people.

While working at JB for my fellowship, I put together packets of information about peer support. It was a pretty new concept at the VA. Before me, there were two veteran's peer supports: Matt and Kenny. They were already busy working with homeless veterans and were assisting them with housing. My job was to get other workers and let the program manager know about peer support and how we could help out our fellow veterans. Week after week, my symptoms of PTSD continued to decrease. I was still working nights at the post office and then doing the fellowship from 7:30 a.m. to 3 p.m. I was learning more about PTSD and was able to connect with other veterans who were having some of the same difficulties. I learned by helping out my battle buddy that I was able to help myself because I did not have as much time to just concentrate on me. The funny thing is . . . the more people I did help out, the better I felt about myself.

Towards the end of my fellowship, I wanted to do some research and see if they had any veteran student groups on the Washington University in St. Louis campus. I did some research and it looked like the Brown School did not have one. I was going to save the last part of my fellowship for when I started attending school and see if there were any veterans or people interested in veteran issues. I wanted to start a student veteran group.

Towards the middle of August, my fellowship was winding down. I worked the fellowship about 30 hours per week from March 2008 to August 2008 and people saw it in a big way of how I carried myself. I talked to some of The Mission Continues board members who I am pretty good friends with now and they said that I was a totally different person than when I first started my fellowship. I was part of a team again, had a purpose of helping out my fellow veterans, and challenged myself in new ways, such as public speaking and facing rejection trying to get the word out about The Mission Continues. I tried to set a good example for my little guy Timmy Jr. and be someone he could be proud of.

Another great day for me was June 30, 2008, when Terri had our second son Tyler at Missouri Baptist Hospital. I was so excited and proud to be a dad again. My Aunt Mary was our delivery nurse and she did a great job. Tyler did not want to come out and was being stubborn. My Aunt Mary and some other nurses worked with Terri and she did not have to have a c-section. Tyler came out a healthy 8-pound boy and I was so happy. I could not wait to be his dad and teach him whatever I could. I felt so fortunate because now I was going to have two sons. I was so pumped about that and they both mean the world to me.

It was the middle of August 2008 and I had just finished my fellowship at the Department of Veterans Affairs. The VA thought I did a very good job with my fellowship, so they hired me full time. I was working as a peer support counselor at the VA from 7 a.m. to 3:30 p.m. and would attend night classes three to four days a week at the Brown School of Social Work at Washington University in St. Louis. I still could not believe I got into a school like that. Started at Affton High School, Forest Park Community College, St. Mary's College, UMSL, and then Wash U was a big change for me. I remember walking into the Brown School—it looked like a medieval castle. I was 29 years old at the time and most of the students were probably about 23 or 24 years old. The first day of school, we had an orientation in a round theatre. VA Voc Rehab was paying for my entire education and books, but my stipend money for notebooks did not kick in yet. I remember sitting by myself in the middle of a row. A few minutes later, I took out a green army PMCS (Preventive Maintenance Check System) notebook. I heard a voice above me whisper, "Damn son, you can't afford a regular notebook," and start laughing. His name is Timothy Fitzpatrick and he was a Navy Veteran for 15 years and an Army Veteran for six years and had been deployed to Afghanistan. Ever since that day, Tim and I were battle buddies and looked after one another. Monica told us there was another Iraqi Freedom Veteran named Shakeya Calloway. She was a semester ahead of us. It was nice to be able to talk to people who were in similar situations and could understand where we had been.

I worked very closely with Monica and I owe her a lot. My writing skills at first were really lacking and she would proofread all of my papers. Believe me, there were a lot of red marks. Some of the papers that I typed would be about 25-30 pages and I did a lot of research. My primary focus was mental health with a specialization in management. I was really excited about the information I was learning like I had never been before. The information I learned helped me personally deal with the symptoms of PTSD, and I could share information with my other brothers and sisters who might have had the same struggles. The first semester was probably the hardest for me, but I was doing very well. I worked very hard, but the learning was addicting.

To me, this was not school that I had to attend. It was a school that I was fortunate enough to be able to attend, and there are many people who would love this opportunity I had. I was learning more about my colleagues and they were learning more about me. Most of the students that attended the Brown School were high achievers and came from a wealthier background. Coming from a middle-class background and not having always been a high achiever, I kept a wall up at first. Tim, Shakeya, and I were pretty tight, but I knew in order to get the full experience, I had to open up a little bit.

The next semester, I founded Stand United for Veterans at Washington University in St. Louis. I had to fill out about 20 pages of information and that was the first time I ever formed something like that. Tim and Shakeya were my co-chairs and Monica was our sponsor. It required a pretty good amount of attention to detail to fill out all the forms and have our group recognized by the Brown School. Our mission was to have a group where veterans doing their MSWs and who were interested in veteran topics could attend a group meeting once a month. A good number of students were very interested in working with veterans. We usually had anywhere from 15-35 students attend the monthly meeting where our student budget would buy us pizza and beer. The guest speakers from the VA were always a big turnout because working at the VA was a great job. The biggest, most valuable lesson I learned from Stand United for Veterans is that I just imagined it and, eventually, it became reality. That is a life lesson I will never forget; you can see things first in your mind and then can make that a reality.

Tillman Foundation Scholar: Living Pat's Legacy of Service

I heard that the Pat Tillman Foundation was awarding 35 scholarships to those attending undergrad or grad school while being a positive asset in the community to honor. Pat Tillman played for the Arizona Cardinals and then joined the Army Special Forces. Pat was killed in action by friendly fire in Afghanistan and there was a lot of media attention tied to his case and what happened. My understanding is that his wife Marie Tillman started receiving checks and was not sure what to do with it. She then started the

Pat Tillman Foundation to honor his legacy.

I filled out the application to help assist me with childcare. Timmy Jr. was about three years old and we just had another son Tyler who was about five months old. We were so excited when Tyler was born, and he was a great addition to our family. He is the most loving and caring person I know and really wants to help people. At that time, Terri was working at United Healthcare where she was an information specialist and worked on the phones and talked about insurance. The Tillman scholarship I was awarded was for $2,500 a semester, and that helped us out tremendously. Childcare cost for working parents is pretty high and the Tillman Foundation would cover this for us for close to two years. That was a huge weight off Terri's and my shoulders as we were able to concentrate on family, work, and school while living with Aunt Mo. Things were finally starting to come together after receiving my Honorable Discharge about three years prior.

The first class of Tillman Military Scholars consisted of about 40 veterans or family members of veterans. It is an honor to be a part of the Tillman Foundations because these guys and gals that won the scholarships have done some incredible things. It was a wide array of service members with all different military skills that have been able to accomplish a lot in a short period of time. I would kind of smack myself in the wrist wondering if this was a dream. I was excited when I started junior college and now, I was in a class full of veterans where a good percentage of these guys and gals went to Ivy League Schools.

They had all of us Tillman Scholars come together in Washington, D.C. in 2009 and we were put up for three days at the University of Maryland. It was an awesome experience because we were all a part of the military coming together from all over the U.S. None of us had any idea who the other person was but, because we had the same similar experience of the military, we became close in a very short amount of time. The Tillman Foundation brought some great speakers to talk to us about leadership. After we listened, we would break up into groups and practice different leadership scenarios. I remember filling up my notebooks with different leadership styles and real-life examples of how people led in the past. This was a very big honor because we would be living Pat's legacy. He turned down millions of dollars to serve his country. He is the definition of selfless service. That leadership summit was great and re-energized me. I know how extremely blessed I am to have been able to attend different leadership summits like that. Looking back, the scholarship helped out immensely at the time my family needed support and to get us back on our feet.

What I have come to realize is that the network of people was just as important as the scholarship, if not more important. There are now over 600 Tillman Military Scholars all over the U.S. We are like family and only a phone call away. It is pretty cool, thinking about the different opportunities because we want to help each other out, so we can make our communities better. I am still very involved with the Tillman Foundation and it has been a life-changing experience.

Meeting the U.S. President: A Moment of Honor and Recognition

Because of the fellowship with The Mission Continues, I had the honor to meet former Commander in Chief, President George W. Bush in 2008 in front of Air Force One at St. Louis Lambert International Airport, with the founder of The Mission Continues Eric Greitens.

About three weeks prior to that meeting, I got a call from the White House Security Team asking if I was Timothy J. Smith. I answered yes and they explained why they were asking. At first, my heart dropped and I wondered why the President of the United States of America's private detail was looking at my background and vetting me. I gave them all the information they asked for and they explained that they would contact me in two weeks. I said great, still kind of in a haze about what took place. I called Eric's office to ask him about all of this. He said pretty cool huh? We get to spread the word about The Mission Continues and meet President Bush.

About three weeks later, Eric, I, and another Mission Continues fellow were on our way to meet the President at Lambert Airport in St. Louis. Talk about an adrenalin rush—my heart was pounding on the way to the airport. I remember thinking in my mind, just keep walking straight and don't slip and fall. I know that seems pretty simple, but it was going to be televised on all of the local news channels. The President's security detail team had us follow them in a warehouse. We saw the presidential limo and his motorcade parked inside the warehouse. We had special access areas because we had to wait about two hours before Air Force One touched down. The presidential detail was pretty stern at first, because they have to be. After they found out Eric, I, and another fellow were going to meet the President, they started to talk to us when we were alone.

It seemed a few of them were also veterans and thanked us for our work with the veteran community. Among veterans, there is always that special bond which brings us together where we can connect with each other easily. I remember one of the agents telling me, just go out, and have a good time; the President is looking forward to speaking with you guys. Eric was steady as a rock and just told us to be ourselves and have fun. We are representing our fellow veterans and what we can do in our communities to serve again. Eric is a true leader because, in any situation, he can see the short and long-term goals. Our mission that day was to meet the President and talk to him about what we were doing now as veterans to help others.

While we were on the tarmac, I was looking at all the camera crews that were waiting for Air Force One to touch down. It was pretty intense, and you could see the President's security detail team scanning the entire area and the few people that had passes to be there. I remember hearing Air Force One and then we saw it descending. I was thinking to myself, take this moment in and have some fun. After a few minutes, Air Force One and President George W. Bush were on the ground and President Bush was making his way out of Air Force One. We started following the security detail and we were able to stand in front of Air Force One. President Bush made his way down the stairs and shook each of our hands. He knew our names and thanked us for our service and said he loved being our Commander in Chief. He asked about our deployments and what we were doing for our communities. Eric and I each told him our story and he awarded us with the Presidential Coin and said he was proud of us. He was very personable and had a big smile on his face. We posed for some pictures that the White House staff took. It was an awesome experience—no matter what your personal beliefs are of President George W. Bush, it was still an honor to meet him. I was able to speak with him for five minutes, he seemed very genuine, and it was a true honor to be recognized.

I drove home and I stopped by a Schnucks to buy some flowers for Terri. We watched the news and you could see us in a circle, talking to the President. As a family, we watched it and I remember me saying my biggest fear is that I would trip and fall. I managed to stand straight, and it was an awesome experience. Two weeks later, I received an official package from the White House. President Bush wrote me a handwritten letter and signed the pictures of us. Someday, I will pass those items down to my sons Timmy and Tyler, and hopefully, they will pass them down to their children.

Tim (center) meeting President George W. Bush at St. Louis Lambert International Airport

PATRIOT

COMMERCIAL CLEANING

7

The Entrepreneurial Journey

Founding Patriot Commercial Cleaning: Building from the Ground Up

It was 2010 and I was sitting in a Social Economic Development Class at the Brown School of Social Work. It was about 8 p.m. at night, and I was listening to our professor talk about all the jobs getting outsourced in the U.S. As I was sitting in that class, I saw a custodian pushing his cart outside of the classroom. All of a sudden, I had an idea: why not start a commercial cleaning company where veterans could go to school during the day and work as part of a team at night?

I wrote in my notebook *Patriot Commercial Cleaning*. I really liked that name. The rest of that class, I was jotting notes to myself about cleaning schools and office space. I was not a business major, but I really wanted to help out my fellow veterans and family members of veterans. I will never forget that night because, if I had not been sitting in that class and talking about the shortages of jobs, I don't ever think I would have had the idea. They say that it is very hard to hear your calling and I totally agree. I was about 31 years old and it was like a perfect storm. Seeing the custodian was what put the icing on the cake—it made sense since most office space and schools would be cleaned at night. It would be cleaned at night when there were not as many people around, and it would be cleaned for the next morning.

My last semester, I had to write a business plan for one of my leadership courses. I had never written anything close to a business plan besides when I started the Stand United for Veterans group at the Brown School. I went to see my friend Darcella Craven, who is the Executive Director at Veterans Business Resource Center. It was about 20 pages, and you just answered the questions by doing your research. I really got into writing the business plan. I heard a saying one time, "How do you eat an elephant?" The answer is one small bite at a time. I was able to bounce ideas off of my wife Terri; it was great to have her thoughts involved. I did not feel alone during the process.

At the time, my dad, Jim, was working 3 a.m. to noon at TSA doing airport security. I would also email him to ask for his thoughts. He worked over 25 years in a factory making food products and has a lot of operational experience. I think it brought us together even closer because it was like when I was a kid and my dad coached me. We were back in the game, getting ready to compete—only in a different game this time around. Honestly, none of us had any idea what we were doing, but had a great time just thinking, "What if we could make this happen?"

I was working at the VA at the time, from 7 a.m. to 3:30 p.m. and then would go to grad school at night on Mondays, Wednesdays, and Fridays from 5:30 p.m. to 9 p.m. I would get up at about 4:30 a.m. and start to write the business plan. It was very early but I had so much energy because of the excitement. This was only an idea at the time but page after page of filling out the business plan, I could see it could happen and there is a need to clean office spaces and veterans need an opportunity to work to be a part of a team. The final business plan was 27 pages long. It was pretty thorough. Five and a half years later, I will say that the business plan was essential, but only about 35% of it was accurate. What I found out is that a lot of the things I thought would work did not and some of the things I thought would not work did. It is a very exciting process because you are making something out of nothing.

In December 2010, I graduated from the Brown School of Social Work and found myself having some extra time at night. What should I do now? On January 1, 2011, I officially launched Patriot Commercial Cleaning. My first customer was a Vietnam Veteran who owned an insurance agency. His name is Larry Abrams and his wife was Carol Abrams. They are one of the nicest couples that I have ever met who are passionate about helping veterans. Larry is a Vietnam Veteran who wanted to help the younger generation of veterans have a better homecoming and more opportunities compared to what they had.

Challenges of Small Business: Grit, Growth, and Hard Lessons

I remember the first night like it was yesterday. Terri was watching the boys while my dad and I went to clean the office. We started top to bottom—dusting, taking out the trash, vacuuming, disinfecting restrooms, cleaning the kitchen, and a few other things that needed to be done. We had a great time and smiled a lot because we had our first customer. From my experience, getting your first customer is the hardest thing to do. I will always be very appreciative to Larry and Carol for giving me the opportunity.

Four months later, I was cleaning two buildings at night, so I was able to hire my first team member and good friend Willie Mathis. Willie was a fellow peer supportive veteran with me and had a lot of stripping and waxing floor experience. Willie was an Army veteran who was in during the Vietnam era. He showed me the right way to strip and wax floors and was very knowledgeable. I hired him and he started cleaning Senior Scripts and was in charge of all our project work. He did a great job and was always very reliable. I felt very fortunate to have him as a teacher and to this day, he is a very good friend of mine.

In 2011, we had four accounts and we were able to hire three team members. It was very cool to see this happening because it all just started with a thought. I started Patriot Commercial Cleaning with $2,500 that I borrowed from my Thrift Saving Plan, which was basically my retirement. My friend Tony Bryan asked if he could see my business plan. I emailed my business plan to Tony and he told me his friend John Niekrash from Work Vessels for Veterans would like to see it. John really liked the business plan and Work Vessels for Veterans helped veteran startups to get up and going. They awarded me with $3,500 to help pay for my insurance and equipment. They also donated a van to me, so I could move my equipment to different job sites. They were instrumental when we were first starting out, and I will always be appreciative for the help.

Balancing Act: Blending Family Life and Business

In 2012, The Mission Continues asked me to swear in 100 fellows at Wrigley

Field. The coolest thing is that the St. Louis Cardinals played the Cubs that day. They asked me a few weeks before the next orientation class. I was stoked because I would get to hang out with 100 OIF and OEF Veterans, do a service project, and watch the Cards vs Cubs rivalry. I was fortunate enough to bring my wife Terri there with me. The first day when we arrived, we checked into the hotel and we were able to talk to some of the fellows. When you are speaking to other veterans, most of the time, you don't have that awkward moment when you are not sure what to ask them. You just ask them what branch of service they were in and then go from there with the conversation. The day before I swore in the other fellows, Terri and I were able to visit Wrigley Field and I was able to walk on the actual field with about five Mission Continues staff. I was allowed to stand on home plate and I could not believe I was standing in the stadium. It was pretty empty, and it felt nice to take it all in. I never could have imagined as a kid from St. Louis, I would be speaking in front of 45,000 fans at the Cards vs Cubs game. They gave me a microphone and it took a little practice to get used to speaking in the stadium. After you speak, you have to wait a few seconds because of the echo. I had never spoken at a venue that big, so it took me about five times before I felt comfortable.

After I was done practicing, Terri and I went on a boat ride on Lake Michigan. It was a great time just relaxing with Terri and taking in the sights. I was very nervous, but the water was calming and we just took it all in. I remember when Terri and I were 19 and 18, we would go to the Riverfront in downtown St. Louis and look across the river and watch the barges. I am lucky to have someone like that to share my dreams with. I can only hope that my sons, Timmy Jr. and Tyler, feel the same love for someone. I believe they will; they will just have to find that special person. The next morning, I woke up at about 6 a.m. so I could do my morning jog. I always feel better after my run and think better. It frees my mind and I can think clearer.

Three hours later, we were getting ready on the bus to watch the Cards vs Cubs. When we got to Wrigley Field, the Cubs organization brought all 100 of us fellows into a room upstairs. We all got to know each other for about one day and were joking around and having fun. It was almost like I was a kid again, getting ready for a big game. I had butterflies in my stomach and was very nervous and excited. It is feelings like these, when you know you are alive and living life. I think sometimes you have to put yourself in uncomfortable situations to really test yourself. I remember I was standing in front of the doorway, giving high fives to the fellows because they were making their way to the outfield. Luckily, my wife Terri was able to stay with me and talk so we just took it all in. A few minutes later, Terri and I, along with a few Mission Continues staff, went down to home plate. It was a very cool experience because you could see Wrigley Field getting packed. Steve Harvey was down by the bullpen, walking around and talking to Cub players and fans.

Twenty minutes later, the stadium was packed, and I was about to swear in the fellows with The Mission Continues pledge. The fellows made their way across the outfield wall. Once they were lined up, I looked at all of them. It was a very surreal experience because Wrigley Field was so crowded. I started swearing them in and it took about one minute. We nailed it. We all got a standing ovation and it was the loudest that I ever heard; 47,000 fans at Wrigley field thanking us for our service. The Chicago Cubs fans were very professional and very kind. That being said, I am a die-hard Cardinals fan—and the Cards won that game.

Lessons in Leadership: Growing Through Service

2011 was Patriot Commercial's first year in business. It was a great experience turning our idea into an actual business that employed veterans while making money. The first year, we did $23,500 in business. I guess that is not bad because I had a full-time job during the day and we were just cleaning at night.

For me though, it was more about feeling alive. Ever since I was a little kid, I loved to compete. First, it was sports, then it was serving in the military, now I get to play the great game of business. For me, it is like playing *Survivor* in real life. If you don't have a quality service, the marketplace is going to kick you out like in *Survivor*, when you get thrown off the island.

One of the hardest parts for me was learning how to bid, where we make our profit margins and win the job. We are not the highest, but we are not the cheapest either. We are in the middle, but I think we add a lot of value to our customers. Everybody always talks about helping the veteran community or puts a bumper sticker on their car. We actually hired three veterans on staff that year and it was a great feeling. My dream was starting to become a reality. In 2011, Inc. 500 heard about Patriot Commercial Cleaning and our mission to hire veterans and family members of veterans.

Inc. 500 called me about three weeks prior to honoring the top 1,000 small businesses in the U.S. They wanted to profile Patriot Commercial Cleaning and talk about my service and what I was doing now. I was stunned to get that call. The businesses that were attending were doing between one million dollars and 90 million dollars in gross revenue. The Inc. 500 set up a program for military entrepreneurs. They wanted to give back to the veteran community and it started in 2011. They would sponsor 30 veterans to attend the Inc. 500 conference free of charge. They provided mentorship for us and paired us with a mentor who is very successful to help coach us and answer any questions that we had. The awesome thing is these entrepreneurs really wanted to help us and they are passionate. They wanted to see us succeed because I feel they are warriors like us. In the military, we watch each other's back and look after one another. Entrepreneurship is very hard—and you must have thick skin. Every day, you have to earn business and work your ass off. I feel like I have three families: my biological family, military family, and Inc. 500 family. At the awards ceremony, they talked about PCC for five minutes and showed some pictures from my military service and the mission of Patriot Commercial Cleaning. I walked up on stage in front of 2,500 entrepreneurs. They gave me a standing ovation and it was like my world stopped.

I talked for about one minute and I was so grateful. I never expected the idea I had for my business would be applauded by the entrepreneurs in our country. At the party afterwards, my buddy Rick Schumaker, who is a Pat Tillman military scholar, and I had a great night. I collected a lot of business cards that night and people were so kind. It was a great night and I even won some new business from that night. I can honestly say that Inc.

500 really cares about the veteran population and wants to help us become better entrepreneurs. I look forward every year to attending GrowCo and the event at the end of the year where they honor the fastest growing companies. I encourage everyone that is interested in entrepreneurship to read the magazine and attend the conferences. You will come back home full of ideas and invigorated.

Patriot Commercial Cleaning Scales

In 2011, we were approached by some gentleman who wanted to help out and set up a voluntary board. They were Kevin Miqueleon, Matt Fagin, Mike York, Pat, Jim Smith, Rob Curcuru, and Alex Curcuru. We met once every three months and it was an awesome group of guys who really wanted Patriot to be successful. Rob and Alex Curcuru are my cousins. Rob is a great salesman with a lot of experience and he always knows his product. He is like a brother to me because he is only a year younger and we always played together since we were kids. Alex is my younger cousin who is a tax lawyer now and was there from the beginning to give us tax advice. Kevin has a lot of experience in startups and has grown businesses in the past, and he is passionate about business. Matt has a ton of experience in commercial office space and he really wants to support the veteran community. Mike has been in the commercial cleaning field for over 20 years and is very knowledgeable on how to bid jobs and the best practices of cleaning. My dad Jim has over 25 years of experience in operations from working in the food industry warehouse. John Scariot works for MasterCard and has some great ideas when it comes to sales. Pat is a small business owner and great with numbers, which helps when you look at long-term and short-term growth.

We had about six meetings and they were very helpful and we had a great time. I enjoyed everybody on the advisory panel and we all got along very well. We talked about financing, bidding, how to get team members, how to build relationships to get new customers, customer retentions, cash flow, and many other topics that helped me grow as a businessman. I always looked forward to the meetings. We had pizza and beer, and the meetings lasted about three hours. Each time, we would build on from the last meeting. We were very fortunate because we had so many professionals with expertise in many different special areas. It was a well-rounded board and, at each meeting, we had increased sales. As a matter of fact, still to this day, we have some very strong increases in sales and we are going in the right direction.

So, I will break down the sales so that it might help out some other small businesses. The first year, 2011, we did $23,400. In 2012, we did $187,000. In 2013, we did $287,000. In 2014, we did $387,000 and in 2015, we did $525,000 in gross sales. In 2016 we did $687,000.00, 2017 we did 835,000.00, 2018 $966,000, and in 2019 we were on track to do about 1.3 million dollars in gross revenue. It has been a very rewarding experience that is very difficult but I love the challenge.

It is definitely a journey and learning experience when you are growing a business. What you think will work does not; sometimes, what you think will not work might actually work beautifully. At the end of 2012, some of the board members approached me and asked if I was interested selling 49% of my company. I was excited; it was hard to believe that people wanted to buy into a company that started with $135.00 in gross sales a month. The guys who wanted to buy into Patriot were familiar with our business model and our mission. They were on board 100% and really did want to help out the veteran community.

I asked my mentor Norm Brodsky, whom I had met at the Inc. 500 and was fortunate to become friends with. Norm and I talked and he introduced me to a life plan. That plan had me and my wife look at our life one year, three years, five years, and ten years out. And so on. We have two great boys, Timmy Jr. and Tyler, who are awesome and whom I love so much. I am not sure if they would ever have any interest in the business, but if they do, I wanted to give them an opportunity to be a part of it. If not, that is great also. I just want them to follow their dreams and work hard. If they are passionate about whatever they do, I will feel like I have done my job as a father. After speaking with Norm, Terri and I wrote down our life plan and where we wanted to be in one year, three years, five years, and so on. That lesson was very valuable and served us well.

I went back to St. Louis after the conference, called the guys, and agreed to hear the pitch. More than anything, I just wanted the experience of going through the beginning of the process when it comes to selling some of our business. Remember, I am educated as a social worker, but it was formal education, so I never learned about evaluations in school. We had the meeting; it was four great guys on the advisory panel and I brought Terri and my dad. Honestly, I think I already had my mind made up before the meeting. I already did the life plan and I thought it was too early to sell any portion of the business. I decided to keep 100% of the business. I did not even give a counteroffer because, at that time, I felt like I could grow the business with my staff organically. I met with my friend Kevin at Romano's Macaroni Grill and told him, "Thanks for the offer, but, at this time, I would have to decline." Formal education is good, but life experience is great and real. My advice to any entrepreneur is to get out there and do the business they want to get into. You are going to get your ass kicked a little bit, but that builds character. You will grow and be more successful from that experience.

8

Facing the Ultimate Test: Battling Cancer

Diagnosis Day: The Shock and Fear of the Unknown

Getting back to the very beginning of what made me want to write this book. The test results for the X-ray were positive for a nodule on the right side of my lung. The next step after that was to have my CT scan. It was about one week before my CT scan. My mind was starting to wonder and worry a little bit. I have two sons, Timmy Jr., who was ten years old at the time, and Tyler, who was seven years old, and a beautiful wife, Terri, whom I love more than life.

Luckily, work was keeping me pretty busy and we had just won two new cleaning contracts which was good. I learned from dealing with PTSD that you have to stay busy and focused. One of the toughest times for me was not having a job for six months when I first got out of the service and thinking about issues that I had over there and different scenarios I could not have changed. Maybe a lot of veterans feel that sense of guilt and it is very hard to talk about. When you see your buddies the day before, and then they are killed in action the next day, that wears heavy on your heart. I was doing my job that I was assigned, pulling guard duty that day, but it hurts really bad when you find out eight of your battle buddies were blown up by a vehicle-born improvised explosive device (VB-IED). I remember going to the VA and talking about some of the situations we were in at FOB St. Michael. I try to employ these strategies now while dealing with this.

January 2016

Two weeks later, I had the CT scan and PET scan and they showed that it was most likely cancer in my right lung. The next stop after that was to get the biopsy to confirm and that was another week later. It was the beginning of baseball season, so Terri and I were busy taking the boys to baseball practice. I coached Timmy Jr and Tyler in basketball and in baseball. I helped out whenever I was needed. It is always fun getting out there with the kids, playing ball and hopefully teaching them life skills for the future. I like sports because they teach you not to give up and even if you lose today, you get back up and can win the next day.

About a week later, I went to get that biopsy done. I remember getting wheeled into the room. The doctor gave me a cover to use and then they gave me some medicine. I was knocked out for about 15 minutes. I help coach my son Tyler's basketball team and all the coaches were going to play that night after practice. I had been looking forward to playing that game for about a month. I could not play that night because they did the biopsy; they had gone into my right lung to see if the nodule was cancerous or not. I did not go to Tyler's practice that night because I knew how bad I would want to play in the game.

Another reason I did not go was because all the guys knew I played ball. At the time, only my wife Terri knew what was going on. I did not want to tell anyone because, at that time, it could have still been benign. I figured why worry my friends and family; everybody has enough on their plates already. The day before I got my test results, I went to my mentor and good friend, Eric Greitens. I set up an appointment with his executive assistant, Krystal. By now, we'd known each other for a long time, so she put me on his schedule. Around noon, I told Eric what was going on. I had not told anyone at that time but Terri. I started breaking down a little because I had been keeping everything bottled in. Eric stood up and said, "Give me a hug, brother." Eric helped me out very much through The Mission Continues fellowship. We had been very good friends for eight years. We trusted each other, and I felt comfortable talking to him about what was going on. He thought I was taking the right actions and we talked about life for ten minutes.

The next day, Terri and I went to see my pulmonologist Dr. Ojile. We had about five minutes to wait for the results and it was a very long five minutes. When the doctor came in, he shook my hand and told me, "Here is where we are at. The right nodule is cancerous." I turned as white as Casper the Ghost. It hit me hard, but I was able to keep my composure. I knew I had another big fight coming up. In my mind, I was almost going back to the time before I went to Iraq. I tried to stay very focused and make sure I was going into this with the right state of mind. After the appointment, Terri and I went over to my parents' house. This was one of the hardest moments of my life. I never wanted my mom and dad to worry about me. While I was in Iraq, when I did call them, I always told them everything was fine. It is not like they could have done anything about it anyway. I always figured, why put extra stress on your loved ones when they couldn't do anything about it anyway? I walked in the door and said, "Hi." They asked me what was wrong. I put my coat in my 'old room', which is now what we call the deer room because my dad shot a buck and that is where it is mounted. I walked in there and I could hardly get it out of my mouth. I said, "I have lung cancer in my right lung," and broke down. I felt like I was letting my boys, my wife, and my parents down. They gave me a big hug and I said that I was going to be okay. "They found it early and I can get it operated on." It is a scary thing to have happen to you, but you have to remain positive and keep the faith. This was just another obstacle—and I was ready to tackle it. Like I said earlier, I was blessed with a very tight-knit family and we always look out for one another.

The doctor told me that, in two weeks, I was going to have 25% of my right lung removed. At the time, I was thinking to myself, "Just do what you have to do to get this cancer out of me." I did not tell anyone but Terri, mom, dad, Eric, and a few close friends. I could not talk about it without getting a little emotional, I have always kept that very close and did not talk a lot about it. I was doing the elliptical for 50 minutes a day and was training hard. The doctor told me, the better shape I was in, the easier recovery would be. About two days before I went into the operation, I posted about what was happening on Facebook. I wanted to warn other veterans that were in Iraq and Afghanistan to make sure they get their lungs checked out. We were exposed to a lot of burning trash, titanium in the dust, and put IEDs in a five-ton so they could be disposed of.

There is research saying that over a thousand veterans who served in Iraq and Afghanistan were having some issues with their lungs because of the environment. In all actuality, I was lucky that I had that cough. If I had not had that cough, I would not have known about the cancer in the top right of my lung. The Facebook post got a lot of attention and the next day, I received a call from Paul Schankman, from Channel 2 news. He heard about the burn pits in Iraq and wanted to ask me about them. We did a five-minute interview and it was the cover story at 6 p.m. My hope was, again, that it would encourage veterans and doctors to get an X-ray to test for this. God works in mysterious ways. I was very fortunate to catch this early. I am very thankful that He was giving me the option to fight; that's all I ever wanted, an opportunity to fight this.

The next day was St. Patrick's Day and I would usually be celebrating with all my friends in Dogtown. This St. Patrick's Day, I was going under the knife so they could remove 25% of my right lung. My wife thought St. Patrick's Day would be a lucky day; I agreed with her because I am Irish. I slept okay the night before and, pretty soon, it was 6 a.m. and time to get up. I had a lot of thoughts running through my mind the morning of the operation. I woke up and spoke to my boys, Timmy Jr. and Tyler about how great of a day at school they would have. I did not want to show that I was a little uneasy, but I am sure they could tell. I gave them a hug and kiss and told them I love them and am proud of them. I could tell they were nervous, so I told them, "Sometimes, life is going to knock you down. The important thing is getting back up." I assured the boys I would talk to them the next day.

Two hours before the operation, my wife Terri and I were hanging out with my mom, dad and Aunt Mo, who had come up to see me. Being a parent now, I could imagine how nervous they were. I told them, "I will be okay and see you in a little while." They gave me some medication and then they called me into the operating room. I remember I was talking to the doctor about how proud of my boys I was and the next minute, I was out like a light. Apparently, they operated for three hours; of course, I don't remember that. After the operation, I heard someone call my name. I woke up slowly, but surely I was in a daze and was going to be in the ICU the next day so they could monitor me.

They cut in my back, right between my ribs, so they could remove the portion of my right lung. I was very sore, and the scar is now about 19 inches long and, at the time, it was very swollen. I was pumped full of pain medication, so I was not sure what was going on. Then Terri came in to see me. I was so happy and gave her the biggest smile I could, which was probably not much. It was great to see her though and I felt better.

The next day, they moved me out of the ICU and into my room. Terri brought the boys by and that made me feel even better. Every breath I took was so painful, so they had me hooked up to a breathing machine. I was going to have to learn how to breathe again with only 75% of my right lung. I was up to the challenge though. Later that day, I was able to walk three minutes with a walker. I remember I had the loudest walker on my floor. The average age of the floor was about 73 years old. Some of the older patients would hear me coming with my walker and say, "Here comes the young gun, watch out," and then start to snicker a little. I was in the hospital for four days. Each day, I would walk a few more laps around the floor. The last day I did not need the walker anymore, so I figured I was going in the right direction. The doctor said the wound was healing very well and that I could be released. I was excited but still in a lot of pain. I was taking pain pills every three hours for the first ten days, including the first few days at my house. I could not leave my room much. I did start walking in my neighborhood, first for five minutes, then seven minutes, nine minutes, and so on.

I felt better about myself because I could see progress even though it was very small. At least, I was going in the right direction. My buddy Charles Dayton, who was an officer in my unit, came by to see me. Charles and I were at FOB St. Michael at the same time in 2004. Charles lived in the upper half in the old Chicken factory while I lived on the lower half in the tents with plywood and sandbags to take some of the impact from RPGs and mortar rounds. While deployed over there, we did not know one another because he was attached to 2-6 Infantry at the time and I was in 4-27 FA. I was a PFC and at the time, Charles was a 2nd Lt. We met at a meeting for our student veterans group in 2009 at Washington University in St. Louis. We met for coffee and were talking about the same places. Towards the end of the conversation, I asked if he was in 4-27 FA; he laughed and said yes. That moment brought us both very close because we knew the same people and were in the same battles. Small world. I would never have thought a meeting at Kayak's Coffee would bring two guys together that went through some of the same stuff five years earlier. Charles is a great guy with an awesome wife and four great kids. We have been good friends ever since we met that morning for coffee.

Another good friend that came to see me a few days after the operation was my mentor and friend Eric. He saw the scar and said, "Man you got a doozy," and kind of cracked a smile. I could tell he was having fun also because he had so much energy when he talked about it. He was glad I was getting some fresh air by getting out. I told him about the first time I thought I might have cancer and he told me that journaling was a very good idea because it helps us get out our thoughts. Eric stopping by encouraged me and I felt reassured. I just had to keep setting short-term goals, measuring them, and accomplishing them. I could tell every day I was getting stronger because my lung was getting stronger. The third day after the operation, I was only able to walk three minutes a day. I built it up by three minutes every day; that does not seem like a lot, but to me, that was progress. I had five weeks to start healing before I had to start chemotherapy. I would walk a little every day and, at times, it was very painful because of where they cut me open. One slight move and it was a stabbing pain in between my ribs.

Usually when I go to the gym, I have my headphones on and am just concentrating on my workout. For those three weeks though, I just really enjoyed my walks and I started talking more with people. There is a group of older people from the ages of 60 to 70 years old who always walk in the morning. I started talking to a few guys that work out in the morning and really enjoyed the conversation. Sometimes, we get so busy because of life, we forget to enjoy the small things. I guess this experience has taught me to, at times, just take a minute and really look at God's beautiful creation.

My first round of chemotherapy was April 18, 2016. My appointment was at 9:30 a.m. and they wanted to get a baseline X-ray of my chest, so they could do a before and after-chemo. After that, they hooked me up to an IV injection and started to infuse me with a lot of different medications. I watched the old school movie sleepers while they were doing the infusion. I did not feel bad during the infusion and was glad to have started the process. I would have to go through four rounds. For the first three days, I did feel run down and did not have much energy. I had to force myself to eat small portions, like, bite sizes of BBQ pork ribs tasted great. After the sixth day, I got my energy up again and started feeling better. I was able to start walking after day seven. Chemo really took a lot out of me for about the first week. I would push myself to get out of bed and get some fresh air. That always helped me feel better. At this time, I would answer phone calls about the business and send emails. Luckily, I have my wife Terri, who would help out keeping up with all the financials and invoices. She really helped me and did a great job.

My dad is our quality manager and would check up on all the properties, making sure we were cleaning to a very high expectation. Luckily, we also had five very experienced veteran team leads. I would communicate with them and make sure they had everything that they needed. We ran our organization like the military—with a chain of command. This cuts down on confusion and makes us more efficient. Everyone knows their role and what is expected to be done. This helps us keep all our customers while growing the business. In the cleaning business, the most important piece is the person cleaning the facility. We learned in the military that if you take care of your soldiers, they will take care of you. I expect a lot from our team members, but I would go through hell and high water to help them anyway I could, as long as it was legal, of course.

Shark Tank Audition

Three weeks after my first round of chemo, I was able to attend the Inc. 500 in Las Vegas, Nevada, again. I always have a great time there. By being a Pat Tillman Scholar in 2009, I was accepted into the Military Entrepreneur program sponsored by the Inc. 500. It is an awesome organization that offers us mentorship and guidance from the fastest growing companies in the U.S. I have learned a lot from attending the conferences and it has really helped Patriot Commercial Cleaning grow.

I was able to bring my dad to this conference with me and we had a great time hanging out. He would hit the casinos during the day and the after-hour networking cocktail hours with me. We would talk about business, and I was able to introduce him to my friends from the Inc. 500 that I have known for about four years. My dad always worked in operations at the bakery, so this gave him insight into the mind of other entrepreneurs. It was nice to get away for a while and try to forget about what I was going through.

The day of the second morning were the *Shark Tank* auditions at our hotel, The Red Rock, on the outskirts of Vegas. I was able to pitch Patriot Commercial Cleaning to Mark Salyers, the executive producer of *Shark Tank*. They listen to over 40,000 pitches a year and only about 250 people get picked to actually go on stage and pitch to the Sharks. From hearing some of the other executives talk in an outbreak session, it seemed like 99% of the time, you need a product and not a service you offer. They explained they took on businesspeople with a project, because they could sell it online to potential customers who were watching the *Shark Tank* episode. Also that project-to-consumers is a lot more interesting than business-to-business. They explained the show is educational but also entertainment, and not as many people find business-to-business as interesting. Plus, then the viewers could not buy as much of the product.

I thought that, when I pitched PCC to Mark, I did a pretty good job explaining our mission to hire veterans and family members of veterans to be a part of a team again, who our customers are, our gross annual revenues, and our plan to scale the business. He explained that what we were doing hiring other veterans was a great thing. I never did get a callback, but it was a very cool experience. What I learned as an entrepreneur is that you have to put out many lines, sometimes you will hook onto something and a lot of times, you won't. You can't get discouraged and down on yourself. Just because your service or product is not right for one person does not mean it's not right for anyone. You have to identify your customer and explain to them that you can solve their problems. I had a great time at that Inc. 500 conference and was able to take some useful notes.

I always get re-energized after attending the conference. This year was a little different though. Our flight got home to St. Louis at about midnight and the next day, I had my second round of chemo. That conference helped keep my mind off everything that was going on and I tried to live as normal as I could for those few days.

Strength and Support: Family and Community Rallying Together

The next morning, my chemo treatment was at 9 a.m. at Missouri Baptist Hospital. I was in very good spirits because I had an awesome time with my dad at the Inc. 500 conference. They loaded me up with IVs and I spent about four hours at the hospital. The next few days, I felt pretty lethargic and beat up, but for me, my fifth and sixth days were the worst. I would vomit up nothing but bile because I could not keep very much down besides popsicles and Jello. It was very aggravating for me and I was stuck in bed or the bathroom. Honestly, I was pretty useless those few days. I was alive, but I was a shell of a person. Eventually on day eight, I started feeling better and would walk a little around Jefferson Barracks Park. I would get up and enjoy watching all the deer walk around like they owned the place. They really do because a lot of times, when I would drive my car there, I would have to wait for a family of three to four deer cross the road.

The last six years, I have been into YouTube-watching while working on different subjects I enjoy. While I was watching, I put in the search "Ways to Cure Cancer." One of the videos was of a patient who had a very large mass and had tried everything. The last thing the patient did was to visit a group of doctors in Japan who cured people by their belief. It was a 15-minute video and the doctor kept saying *Waso*. It is Japanese, I believe, for "I am healing." The doctor kept saying this over and over again. He would say it with conviction, and you could see the mass getting smaller and smaller until it disappeared. I was very impressed and believed this might be able to help me also. When I would walk, I would say *Waso* over and over to myself in my head, that I was healing and feeling better. I would enjoy the beautiful nature while walking and keep saying this to myself at the same time. I believe this method really helped me believe in myself.

The first person I told about potentially having lung cancer, after my wife, was my good friend Eric. I needed someone in my life who would listen to me and would not feel sorry for me but help me problem-solve.

One of the lessons that I learned from Eric was segmenting. I had to break the lung cancer down in smaller pieces because it was pretty overwhelming. The first stage I had to deal with was them removing 25% of my lung and not being able to breathe very easily. I had to break this down into small segments to get through this. Sometimes, on the third or fourth treatment, I had to break it down hour by hour because I got pretty sick at times.

When I was diagnosed with lung cancer, Eric and The Mission Continues helped me build internal confidence. I truly believed I could beat lung cancer. I did not believe myself at times. I was scared and did not know what the future held for me. I learned how to fight through some difficult times, and the saying is true—what doesn't kill you, makes you stronger.

The third round was worse, and the fourth round was the hardest. I think it was because all that medication is in your blood. I could not eat or hold anything down for nine days after the third treatment and 11 days after the fourth treatment. At that time, I was losing about 11 to 14 pounds each time because nothing was in my stomach. I would keep vomiting bile and it was very annoying. I had no energy and felt like I was letting my family down. It was hard to concentrate and it felt like everything was falling apart. I was getting down on myself and could feel myself slipping into a bad place.

In July, we lost two pretty big contracts. The reason we lost them was because we were not doing as well on quality management like we had been in the past. On our cleaning contracts, we ask for 30 days before we part ways on the contract. Honestly, my #1 goal went from growing the company to just surviving and beating the cancer. Losing the business sucked. But I knew I could build it back up, I just had to get healthy. Even when I was struggling, I would tell myself each day that I was getting better.

To make matters even worse, I had borrowed $6,500 from my business line of credit one time for a bigger job we had. I was able to pay it back two weeks later. I was not keeping up with all the mail at that time like I should have. Around April, I started getting some letters that said I owed $65.00 in interest. I figured, it was only $65.00 and I would get around to paying for it sooner or later, so it was no big deal. It turned out to be a pretty big deal because I paid it back in 63 days instead of 60 days. Because of all the regulations the bank has, I lost my $30,000 line of credit. That really hurt, because it was unsecured and gave us the ability to grow as we needed when new contracts came up.

In July, we had a pretty big stripping and waxing job coming up in eight different facilities. I would need about $25,000 in working capital to get the job completed but only had about $50,000 in working capital to pay my team members and other expenses. What I did was pull out about $33,000 from my IRA. I knew that I would be penalized for withdrawing that money, but I could also make a very nice profit margin with that capital in about a month's time from stripping and waxing the floors. It worked out well for me because we accomplished the mission. I would not advise everyone to do this. I was a 37-year-old with lung cancer. My thought process was that if I live to turn 65, that would be awesome, but I am living now and can make some money to help support my family. I was able to roll that money into my savings, and my plan was to buy and rent multi-tenant properties for cash flow.

I had always wanted to get into real estate since I was about 31 years old and started reading Robert Kiyosaki's *Rich Dad Poor Dad*. In three months, I built up capital from $33,000 to about $70,500 just by putting money aside. I was starting to feel more confident because I was growing that account along with the $51,000 in the business operating account. To me, this was a lot of capital because I started out with $3,200 from my Thrifts Savings Plan. After paying all your expenses, such as payroll, equipment, supplies, taxes, and miscellaneous expenses, it adds up. I was proud to be able to do this because it takes strategy, discipline, and some luck to get the opportunities to win new business.

Faith, Resilience, and Recovery: A Journey of Hope and Healing

I will never forget July 5th, 2016. My wife Terri and I were going to the doctor's office to get the CT scan results from the Friday before. Honestly, I was very nervous for the results and so was Terri. This was probably the most uncomfortable that I had felt so far. I think the reason was because

I already had them remove 25% of my right lung and then went through four rounds of chemo that took a lot of out of my body. Eric Thomas says, "If you are going through all of the pain, make sure to get the reward." My reward would be staying alive so I could be there to watch my boys grow up and for the love of my life. I was very fortunate because I had a lot of people saying prayers for me and I will always be thankful.

The test results were negative and I was cancer-free. That was one of the biggest reliefs that I have ever felt. I just hugged Terri and was kind of in disbelief. I had to go through one more chemo treatment and Terri was still not sure of the diagnosis, so while I was getting the treatment, Terri actually went back to the doctor to make sure I was indeed cancer-free. I think she just wanted to hear it again. She came back with a big smile on her face and said, yes, we did hear it correct. Later that day, we were able to tell my parents and our boys. We were all very happy, and I think we all slept better than night. I also used a technique called visualization when the doctor diagnosed me and I started the treatments. When I would walk Jefferson Barracks Park, I would tell myself I feel great and visualize I was cancer-free. I would say it to myself over and over—and I really felt like I was healing. At times though, I did feel self-doubt. I would get scared and think to myself, "What if it does not work?"

Other times, I would shed a few tears when I was alone. I never wanted anyone to worry about me. I could always hide my emotions pretty well; that is not always a good thing because my wife would say sometimes, "You look like you have no emotions." I think when you live through certain things like we did in Iraq, you learn how to not show too much emotion because, at times, it is so painful. You just worry about the mission and keep pushing forward. I am working on that now, but it is still tough because I don't want to feel vulnerable or look weak. What I would do with these feelings is try and watch a motivational video—and push those feelings aside. I was able to usually do this within a few minutes. I already know that life can be difficult, but it does you no good to feel sorry for yourself. You have to look deep inside your soul and find the reasons you are fighting and living for. Once you find out your why, the pieces of the puzzle will start coming together because you have a reason for living.

9

Navigating Money, Business, and Life's Battles

How I Learned About Money and Business

I have previously mentioned the book *Rich Dad Poor Dad* by Robert Kiyosaki. That book opened my eyes to a whole new way about thinking of business. The four main quadrants he talks about are Employee, Small Business Owner, Big Business Owner, and Investor. I would highly recommend it to anyone that is interested in starting a business. I have spent over 50 hours reading about him and how he created his wealth. He invested in himself and his education. He makes a lot of money in real estate and cash-flowing properties. He started out small and built a great portfolio of apartments all over the U.S. The first piece of advice he gives about real estate is to buy in an area that you live close by and that you know. Like anything, there will be a learning curve and at least, if you are close to it, it is easier to deal with issues that come up. Another thing he talked about is you should look over 100 deals before you make an offer. People are selling properties for different reasons and your job is to find the best property for you, where the cash flow is good and you get a good ROI (Return on Investment).

Another speaker I listen to is Grant Cardone. He is another entrepreneur that started off as a car salesman and now is also in real estate. He talks about how you can be obsessed or be average. He talks about how a lot of people do not live up to their potential and they think too small. He believes that people have to 10x their goals. Basically, multiplying by ten. To me, that makes sense because even if you fall short on your goal, at least you are shooting higher and have more opportunity for growth.

I google "motivational YouTube" when I am working out, walking, or driving in my car. This helps me think about how good the world is.

I usually start my work out at about 5:30 a.m. or 6 a.m. Listening to this helps me start my day off on the right foot. Before all of the stresses of the workday, I have already exercised my body and mind. I am learning about issues that can positively affect me and my family. I have always been very good about exercising from playing sports as a kid, but my diet is poor. I eat a lot of carbs, but I am really trying to eat more protein and vegetables. It will be tough, but I am going to set short-term and long-term goals of living a healthier life.

I think once you find a good mentor, and when you find something you love, it becomes addictive. You keep trying to find more information about those people. I hope my sons Timmy Jr. and Tyler find something they are passionate about and go for their dreams. You only live one life, so give it everything you have.

The Gift My Father Gave Me

My dad and I have always been close and he is my hero. From coaching me in basketball as a kid to being my operational manager in Patriot Commercial Cleaning. The biggest gift my dad gave me was that he believed in me. He would always encourage me and know that I would find a way to get it done.

We had two very big bids out in November and in December and I was working hard on closing the deal. It takes a lot of time and effort to close a deal and being able to bounce ideas off my dad is great. Due to my dad always having worked in operations, he often thought differently than I did. I was always very aggressive when it came to sales, which I think is great. On the other hand, I do think you need someone with a solid background in operations so you can execute the plan. We finished the year 2016 very strong; we had four very big projects we were going for and won two out of four. That will bring us an additional $13,500 per month, which will bring our gross sales up to about $56,000 per month to start the year 2017 off. For some people that might be a very large number and for other people, that might be a very small number. The reason why I bring up the numbers is because it is imperative to know them and to be able to tell if your company is making money. I know the numbers like I know my kids' names. I am very interested in them and want to nurture them so they can grow. If I see they are struggling, I try and help them out by giving them the attention they need.

Bouncing Back

In February 2017, we grew our business by $312,000 gross revenue, which is a huge win for us. I will bring you back to how were able to do this because it did not happen overnight. I am going to break down the numbers to hopefully help the small businesswoman or -man. In 2016, our gross revenue was about $517,000. All in all, that was not too bad, considering that 2016 was tough at times.

We closed one deal in February, but I had been working on that deal for about three years. I met the facility manager at a networking meeting and we exchanged business cards. It started off with a business card and email. After that, I would call him about every six months. He would tell me about some of the issues he was having with the cleaning crew. Over time, we were able to grow a relationship and felt comfortable talking to each another. Nothing panned out for 2½ years and, one morning, I got the call to give him another bid. We finally were able to win that contract for about $8,500 a month. It felt good—and now we had to put our team together.

I worked with the Department of VA Voc Rehab Specialist and we were able to hire some veterans as staff. It is always nice to work with other veterans because we have that sense of camaraderie from the service and they know the importance of attention to detail. With this deal, we would be doing $53,500 a month.

In January 2017, I received a call. We had been working on trying to get this contract for about a year. The CFO called me because she received a good reference from a school which we had been cleaning for five years. Those relationships with your customers are huge because if you do really good work, they will be some of your biggest advocates. They will see your work firsthand, and you can pass on their number to facility managers looking to hire you.

This was another private school, and this contract was about $10,700 a month. This will bring our gross monthly gross revenue up to about $64,800 a month, which is the most we ever did a month in recurring revenue. This means every month, as long as we keep doing a good job, we can count on that. We had a few bigger months gross revenue-wise, but those were bigger months because of stripping and waxing floors. We are already on track in March 2017 to do about $777,600 for the year 2017. This is looking like a really good year in business for us. I am mailing 162 pamphlets to private schools all around the Missouri area. By doing this, we might get three or four opportunities to bid. We clean about 38 facilities nightly and about seven of those are private schools that I made sure to put in the pamphlet. We already have a lot of experience cleaning those types of facilities. If we can close one or two of those deals, we could possibly do about $840,000 in gross sales, which would be a pretty big percentage increase.

It seems like business is a numbers game, and you must throw out a lot of lines and follow up. It is a contact sport and a game of touches. They say it usually takes about seven times trying to contact a person before you might get their attention. I believe that, because in our sales cycle, it could take months to years before finally closing the deal. I love my profession and do not consider it a job. I put a lot of hours in but have a great time doing it. I get to work very closely with my wife Terri and my dad, so we also get a lot of family time. I am not saying everything is perfect all the time, because it is not. I do, however, get to spend time with my family who I love deeply, so that is pretty awesome.

The Impossible is Possible

In March 2017, I was inducted into the Affton High School Hall of Fame and I was the second youngest honoree to be inducted. It was quite an honor for me. Twenty years ago, while I was in high school, I don't think anybody saw that coming, including myself. I had a great time in high school, but I did not apply myself very much. My GPA was around a 2.5; just enough to stay eligible to play basketball.

While in high school, I had many friends, but deep inside, I felt alone. It was like living in two different worlds at times. My home was in Affton, which was a probably 95% white working-class, blue collar neighborhood right outside St. Louis City. Then I pretty much went to the Boys Club of St. Louis at least 5 days a week, which is located in Soulard, in the inner city of St. Louis. I went to the Boys Club from 8 to 16 years old, so it played a really big part of my life. It was much grittier up there and I learned to be pretty street-smart, because if you were not, people would take advantage of you. This is why I had the attitude—where no one is going to treat me like I was soft because up there, if you let people treat you like that, you were going to have a miserable existence.

I will say, looking back at all those experiences, I had some great times and some of those guys from the club are my best friends to this day. At the club, we did not see color because it was a very diverse group of many cultures and colors. To get back on track though, I remember one of my high school gym teachers told me in front of the entire class, "Mr. Smith, it is people like you who bring down my property value." The entire class started laughing and I kind of played it off laughing also. But inside, I thought to myself, "Maybe I am just a white boy that could hoop and that was all." I look back at my time then and I really had no self-confidence. I think, at times, teachers label you along with many other people. At the end of the day, it was really because I did not believe in myself.

Now, I was very lucky to have Coach Parker believe in me, along with a few other teachers, which was a very big thing for me. My mom and dad believed in me, but at times, I know I drove them nuts and had them worried. I am pretty stubborn and at that point in my life, I just wanted to play basketball and have a great time. I was able to speak to some of my teachers and my counselor that night and tell them thank you. At one time in my life, I may not have taken their advice, but I always remembered it. Those lessons in life would help me very much in the future, teaching me about character and responsibility.

I would say to all teachers, "First of all, thank you for what you do because your job is extremely important in molding our self-esteem and future. Secondly, you might not see the results of the lessons you taught us in grade school and high school, but believe me, we remember them. They will help us out tremendously in the future because of the seeds you planted in us when we were younger. Just help the younger generation believe in themselves because they might not believe they have self-worth at that time."

Here We Go Again—2019

It was 2019; Patriot Commercial Cleaning was going great and the family was thriving and doing very well. Every six months, I had to go in and do a CT scan. I went to my oncologist, Dr. Lyss, and it looked like the cancer was coming back and spreading again. My heart dropped and all these feelings started coming back again. Dr. Lyss said, "Let's do a trial drug called Tagrisso." I started taking it for one month and my face started to break out terribly. To be honest with you, I really did not care because my goal was to stay alive for my family and I would do whatever is necessary to do that.

This was more mental than physical pain compared to the surgery where they took out 25% of my right lung and had to cut in between my ribs. That pain was excruciating for 6 weeks. After I healed, I had to do four rounds of chemo, which was very hard on my body. With the drug Tagrisso, Dr. Lyss said, "Let's cut it down from 110 milligrams to 80 milligrams." This stopped me from breaking out and was the right amount. The doctor checked the scan two months later and I was in remission, cancer-free again! I have to be honest with you and say that is the sweetest words a person can hear coming from the doctor's mouth. God is great and I believe my faith helps me out tremendously. He has been watching out for me my entire life. I must say, when I was in Iraq in 2004, I got really close to Him, because of all the death and destruction I was around. I remember I would rub my St. Michael medallion that was with my Dog Tags around my neck. That was always very comforting.

Reclaiming a Home and Building a Business

Around 2019, we were renting out our old house in South St. Louis off

Morganford. I went to check on it because the tenant was moving out. I could not believe it—when I opened the door, the smell was horrendous. Our house was totally destroyed! There were piles of dog feces and hubcaps through the entire house. I was in disbelief and felt sick to my stomach. My wife Terri and my two sons, Timmy Jr. and Tyler, walked into the house with me. My boys broke down because they saw their room. They were about 6 years old when they had both shared that room.

It took me a few days to get my mind together and try to figure out how I was going to fix this major issue. I remember going to Home Depot at Kingshighway and Arsenal. I saw a van with ICS and decided to call the number. That is where I met Israel in Aisle 7. I explained to him the problem and what I was looking for. He explained that he could take a look because it was December and St. Louis was cold and snowy at the time. He also explained that he did this work and could help out; that was some good news for me.

I remember the first thing I did was to clean and then hire some team members I already had on the team to help clean the house up. It took four 20-yard dumpsters to finally get all the junk and hubcaps out of the house and garage. Basically, we had to gut the entire house. I would have ordered two 40-yard dumpsters if I had known how much trash there actually was. We had to take out all the fixtures in the house, totally redo the kitchen, bathrooms, and change out the wood floors, then re-sand them and then stain them. The only thing the house had going was it had good bones and was in a decent location.

Eventually, after we had cleaned the house, Israel and his crew started working their magic rehabbing the house. They worked there about two months straight and did a great job. We were fortunately able to sell the house for more than what we owed on the house, so it worked out well and I learned a lot from that experience. I was very happy about the house, and Israel and I had learned to trust one another. He told me his main job was roofing and I was pleasantly surprised. In 2019, I started a roofing company, Patriot Industries, and we did a little bit of patch and repair work to provide Patriot Industries with positive cash flow from doing smaller jobs. I started that company the same way Patriot Commercial Cleaning was started: little by little, without taking out a loan and starting out with debt. My cousin Rob Curcuru and best friend has 17 years of experience in the roofing industry. We work very closely together and it is nice to work with someone you can trust and have a lot of respect for. Rob and I have hung around since he was a few months old. We would hang out ever since we were little kids and had some great times with one another. We can bounce ideas off one another and then we will come up with a plan and move forward. I believe it is very important to find the business first and then start building up a solid customer base. The most important thing I believe when starting a business is doing a great job for the customer and then the word of mouth will grow organically.

Starting in January 2020, I began to truly believe that I was coming into my own as an entrepreneur. Attending a Grant Cardone Business Conference in Las Vegas was a pivotal moment, where I heard incredible speakers like Magic Johnson share their stories. Listening to Magic's journey—how he built a business empire with the same dedication he brought to the basketball court—gave me hope and ignited my own belief that anything is possible. Inspired and determined, I returned to my businesses with a renewed sense of purpose and began to see the fruits of my hard work take shape.

Patriot Commercial Cleaning Gross Revenue and Headcount

- 2019: Patriot Commercial Cleaning (PCC) earned $843,200 with a team of 26 members.
- 2020: PCC reached $947,300 in revenue, growing to 29 team members.
- 2021: PCC saw impressive growth, hitting $1,289,843 in revenue. We rejoined the Entrepreneurs' Organization (EO) that year and expanded to 37 team members.
- 2022: PCC brought in $1,197,248, though the team size decreased to 32 members as hiring challenges arose during the pandemic.
- 2023: PCC earned $1,101,290, with team numbers dropping to 29, as finding the right people remained difficult.
- 2024: PCC is projected to achieve $1,201,297 with 34 team members.

Fortunately, hiring is beginning to improve, and today our workforce is composed of 50% veterans, 30% veteran family members, and 20% individuals who share our core values of hard work and discipline.

Patriot Industries Gross Revenue and Headcount

- 2019: Patriot Industries generated $43,200 in revenue from patch and repair work on flat roofs, with a small team of 2.
- 2020: Amid the pandemic, Patriot Industries pivoted to residential roofing, achieving $294,303 in revenue with a team of 4.
- 2021: Revenue increased to $432,368, as we ventured further into commercial roofing with a dedicated team of 3.
- 2022: Patriot Industries continued to grow, earning $631,297, with an expanded focus on commercial contracts and a team of 4.
- 2023: With $931,202 in revenue, more commercial contracts flowed in, supported by a strong team of 5.
- 2024: Patriot Industries is on track to reach $1,128,287, marking a substantial milestone with a team of 6 as we continue to build our commercial presence.

These numbers were more than just financial milestones; they represented countless hours of dedication, lessons learned, and moments of resilience. Through the highs and lows, my family and team were my constant anchor and inspiration. Not only was I running two successful companies, but I was also witnessing my family life and career flourish in ways that exceeded every expectation I ever had. This journey was both humbling and transformative, proving to me that with persistence, heart, and the right people by your side, you can build a life that's both meaningful and inspiring. I was grateful for the support I've had along the way, and I was excited for all that was yet to come.

September 2024, The Cancer Comes Back Again

This is the fourth time that I have to fight this. They told me it came back in my left lung. Of course, when you get this news, your heart drops and I was like, "Oh shit, here we go again." This time, they suggested that I do chemo. I was going to have to do nine rounds. One round every three weeks. The first week and a half every week after each round, I was very sick. This really beat my body up and took a toll on me, as I am sure it did on the kids and Terri. I did this for about seven months and really hoped that it would work. I took it week by week.

After months of doing the chemo, I had to do the final CT scan. Now, the month is September 2024, and they said the cancer has spread in my lungs, to my liver, and now my brain. The doctors were great and I really appreciate all the help over the years. I have been battling the lung cancer for over eight and a half years. At least I got to watch my boys Timmy Jr., who is now 18 years old, and Tyler, who is now a sophomore in High School, grow up and become teenagers. That is honestly the biggest accomplishment of my life—being able to raise them, coach them, and just be able to spend time with them. The doctor said the only thing that they can do is chemotherapy until I eventually die anyway. They said the cancer, because it is Stage 4, spread too much and that I would have to spend the rest of my life doing chemo with no chance of beating it this time.

That was the toughest news that I had to hear with Terri. Honestly, it has only been two days since they told me. I had to tell my young sons this and it was so hard. How do you tell your young sons that you are dying and that there is nothing else that you can do. Honestly, I am really struggling with this. Then I have to tell my parents who are older, they are about 71 years old and my mom is not in the best health, that their only son is dying and there's nothing they can do. I am planning on telling them in two days but not looking forward to it. I am just planning on living out the rest of my life with gratitude and feeling lucky with how much God has provided me. The more people Terri and I tell, the more it is starting to get real. I have always been a very private person and never wanted people to feel sorry for me. My dream is to get this book published for my two boys and maybe the last thing I can do is show them to never give up, matter how bleak the future looks.

I had a dream a few weeks ago that my Grandma and Grandpa Quinn, along with Grandma and Grandpa Smith, along with many family members that have already passed on, were calling me and we were all having dinner together and having a great time just laughing. Maybe that was a sign because I had the dream before I got the results of the CT scan. I do believe that there is a heaven and I look forward to seeing all my family members up there, along with some buddies that have already passed on. I look forward to seeing my Army buddies up there and thanking them for giving up so much for our freedom that we all hold so close to our hearts.

November 5th, 2024

10

Reflections on Leadership, Gratitude, and Service

Lessons from the Battlefield: Core Values of Leadership

Every morning that I wake up, I thank God for everything He has given me and provided me and my family with. I look at it this way: each day is a gift and you should make the most of it. Over time, I have tried to appreciate each day for what it is and feel all the emotions deep in my veins. Some days are going to be outstanding, where everything is going your way, and everything just falls into place. Really enjoy those days for what they are and take in all the feelings of joy.

Other days are not going to be that way and you might feel a lot of pain and suffering. Try to get the most out of that pain. Like Eric Thomas says, "You are already in pain, get the reward." From my experience, pain can generate a lot of energy. At the time you are suffering, try to channel that feeling into something positive. Easier said than done, of course. But if you are mindful of your emotions, you can do this! You have to try and find the upside with those feelings of anger and sadness. I have been able to do this in several different ways. When I am feeling down, I think about all the service members who paid the ultimate sacrifice. At times, I still think about April 29th, 2004, when I got the word that eight of my brothers were killed in action by a VBIED. I think about their memorial service and how their families must have felt

It is something I never will forget and, at times, I feel like I should have done more. I was on guard duty when it happened, and it is weird because I was not injured. It is crazy thinking and I feel fortunate that I was not injured while I was in Iraq. My eyes, of course, were jacked up with severe chronic conjunctivitis and, sometimes, my eyes looked like two pieces of ham and I could barely see, but so many more soldiers had it much worse than me. When I was diagnosed with lung cancer, I was nervous; who wouldn't be?

Making Dreams a Reality

One of the biggest lessons in life I learned is from this question I mentioned earlier: How do you eat an elephant? I thought about it for a while and answered, "I am not sure." The answer I was given is, "One bite at a time." What I realized from that conversation is that we need to break down any goals that we might have into smaller goals, so that we do not get overwhelmed.

An example of how I did this was when I wrote the business plan with my wife and dad. We broke it into very small pieces. I was writing the business plan for one of my leadership courses in 2010 at Wash U. I asked my friend Darcella Craven, who is the Executive Director at Veterans Business Resource Center. She provided me with a booklet of 30 pages on questions I should ask myself about the business I want to be in. For us, it was commercial cleaning. The booklet contained 16 sections. I broke each section down and gave myself two days to complete each section. That helped me stay focused on the topic and not get overwhelmed. I identified my goal of spending two days on each topic and answer and research all the questions in that section. With each section that I completed, I gained more confidence. I started to become more familiar with the business and future competitors.

After a month and a half, I had a business plan. For my first one, I thought I did a pretty good job. I brought it back to Darcella and she had one of her advisors, who owned a business, look over it. There was a lot of red ink and plenty of questions! At first, I was like, "Damn, I messed up." I met with the advisor and he explained he wanted to be tough on me before I spent any money. Those recommendations came in handy. I had to borrow $2,500 from my thrift savings plan so I had to make every penny count. It helped me out tremendously. Back to my point though. If I did not break those 16 sections into manageable goals, I don't think I would have started. Sometimes, by stepping back, looking at the big picture, and then breaking it down, you gain a lot of confidence that will save you a lot of time and money.

The Winning Mentality

I believe the winning mentality starts in your mind. The mind is very powerful and can help you achieve things you might never thought was possible. What changes our whole life is action. A decision is the first step you need to take. After that comes the commitment when you make things happen and hold yourself accountable. After that, you resolve the issue. Your decision and commitment will help you resolve whatever problem it is you are working on. It might sound simple, but it is very difficult and will take time. However, if you do follow those steps, you can become successful.

Sometimes, believing in yourself and that it can be done is one of the biggest barriers. You can overcome that barrier by positive self-talk. Positive self-talk is when you concentrate on your strengths and you tell yourself, "You can do this." It might sound corny, but it works. If you tell yourself you can hit your goal over and over again by practicing to master your craft, it is possible. What this does not mean to say is, say you play baseball and you really want to hit the ball, so you tell yourself over and over that you can play, but you do not practice at all. I would not expect that you would start hitting the ball because you told yourself there was no action. However, if you took 150 swings a day and you saw the result of you hitting the ball more often, along with the positive self-talk, I think that then you are setting yourself up to be more successful.

I also believe that you must be willing to fail in order to win. It is normal to feel nervous when you are pushing yourself. If you don't feel a little nervous, you are probably not pushing yourself hard enough. Do you remember that feeling when you were a teenager and you were about to call that girl or boy you liked? How were you feeling at that time? Would your heart race faster? Were you excited or nervous? Did you feel alive? I am sure that you did. I think when we become adults, we miss some of those emotions and the feeling of being alive!

When I call on new customers or before presentations, I get those feelings—I feel alive! With those emotions, I am fortunate enough to experience growth in revenues which helps my company's bottom line. It is a win/win for me because I feel alive and we are hiring more veterans and family members of veterans, which also results in more profit. One way I know I am making the right choice is if I feel nervous, that is what I know I must do first. For example, if I get an email in the morning from a customer because our team missed a trash can or did not clean an area as well as we should have, I must address this situation.

After I work out first thing in the morning at about 6 a.m., I shower, eat breakfast, and then I start my day. The first calls I make are always the hardest ones. I do this for two reasons. The first reason is because it puts me more at ease because I am attacking the situation. If I wait, I have more time to think about it and it just makes the situation worse. The second reason is so that the customer knows that I care, and I will address their needs. The customer will have time to explain the problem to me or my team and we will come up with a solution to fix the mistake. To me, that is a winning mentality because you are not ignoring the situation and facing it head on.

How to Build Your Swag

Building your confidence is going to be essential as you grow as a person. I remember when I was first honorably discharged from the Army in 2007, my confidence was extremely low. I was not part of a team anymore and felt extremely alone. I was also struggling with symptoms of PTSD and that made me feel even worse about myself. Here are a few things that helped me over years to build my swag. The first thing you must do is make a decision that you are going to be confident. You must make a commitment and build that muscle. It always helped me to write down that I could achieve my goals. Write them down like you already accomplished them because it is like a self-fulfilled prophecy. You must see yourself achieving the goal and build confidence in yourself before anyone else will believe in you.

A way to build confidence is to find a mentor or somebody you look up to so you can study them and, with the gleaned knowledge, can potentially access many people with different skill sets. If they have a YouTube channel, tune in to their station and follow them. I am a big fan of Grant Cardone; I have read four of his books and watch him on YouTube often. I want to learn more about real estate investing, so I study him. Right now, I only have two properties. One I own, and the other I rent out for $150 a month with positive cash flow. I know that is extremely small, but I must start somewhere. Each month, I put 15% aside for my properties that I am going to invest in. From listening to Grant, I feel much more confident about real estate investing than three years ago. I am also feeling more confident because I am stacking money and will be in a good position to pull the trigger and find the right property in the near future. I am feeling more confident because of the knowledge I am gaining from listening to his podcast and creating a system. Whenever talking to a potential customer or taking on a new venture, people will be able to see from your mannerisms if you are confident in yourself or not. The confidence comes through educating yourself about whatever area your focus is. This will take discipline and commitment to learn your craft and become an expert. However, the payoff can be great because you are putting the time in on the front end.

Another way to build confidence is to have a planner and write down the top seven things you want to accomplish that day—or whatever number is good for you. I always start with the toughest task first and then, when I accomplish one, I put a check mark next to it. I immediately start to feel more and more confident because I can physically see I am getting stuff done and I'm not wasting my time. When this becomes a habit, it will make your life much easier because it becomes instilled in you. They also say you must do something 30 days in a row before it becomes a habit. This can be difficult, but if you are self-aware and measuring it, this will become possible and you will put yourself in a better position to be successful.

In my opinion, the most important kind of thinking is that you can't just drink the Kool Aid, you have to swim in it. The only way that is going to be possible is if you have a lot of confidence in yourself from putting the work in. You have to put in the work if you want to be successful. There is no substitute for hard work! Hard work will build your confidence.

How Wealthy People Think

I have always been fascinated by how rich people think. To be brutally honest, I used to be very intimidated by people who had money. The only reason I might have thought that way is because I grew up in a very blue-collar family and did not grow up around many people that had much money and were wealthy. I had great parents that were great role models for my sister and me, but that did not teach me how to make money. In 2010, before I started my business, I got really interested in Robert Kiyosake and read his book *Rich Dad, Poor Dad*; that is when I started my financial education. I found it very exciting and I learned that 80% of millionaires are self-made. I thought to myself, "This is possible and I can do it." Our business will gross one million dollars this year. This by no means makes me even close to rich or wealthy, but it is a start. When I first got out of the military, I thought $6,000 a year was great, and it is very good. However, I wanted to be able to hire on and help more veterans find employment so I would have to make more money to make that dream possible.

Joining Groups like St. Louis Entrepreneurs Organization and Gateway Insiders Club

I was fortunate enough to join St. Louis EO Accelerator Program in 2014-2016. This was for companies doing $250,000 gross revenue per year. In 2021, I was qualified to join St. Louis EO, which is for companies doing over 1 million dollars of gross revenue per year. I was able to join a forum with six other business owners. We would share experiences that could help us grow the business and also help us out in our personal lives. It is a great organization with some outstanding people and other businesses that are grinding every day. At Gateway Insiders Club, we would meet every 2 weeks on a Friday at the MAC downtown. We would share leads, and that group has some extraordinary business owners and overall just great people to be friends with. I think it is important to join groups like this because *birds of a feather flock together.*

Special Gratitude for The Veterans Business Resource Center

Accountability changes everything—I've seen it firsthand. Being part of a small group at the Veterans Business Resources Center has transformed how I approach my goals. Each month, five of us come together, guided by a skilled moderator who brings in guest speakers to challenge and inspire us. But what I've come to value most is the time we spend in raw, honest discussions, mapping out where we're going and exactly how we plan to get there.

I've learned that writing down what I want isn't just a formality—it's an act of commitment. Setting a target like "secure $7,500 in new contracts for May" means nothing without the objectives to back it up: mailing pamphlets, making follow-up calls, submitting bids. I see now that goals aren't about wishful thinking; they're about taking steady, intentional steps toward something real.

Goal: $7,500 in new contracts for the month of May.

Step One: Mail off 162 pamphlets to potential private schools.

Step Two: Follow up with phone calls to 65 private schools in the 50-mile radius of St. Louis, Missouri.

Step Three: Provide four bids to private schools in the area.

Outcome: Win at least one of those bids that will produce at least $7,500 of gross revenue per month!

Over the past three years, I've been struck by how much our group's diverse perspectives shift my thinking. We work in different fields, but each of us brings something fresh, reframing challenges in ways I wouldn't have imagined on my own. For $250 a year, I'm getting more than just monthly meetings—I'm investing in accountability partners who have become a vital part of my progress.

This shared wisdom has led me to explore other voices and strategies that push my business thinking even further. Recently, I've been reflecting on Jay Abraham's approach: turn your customers into advocates and get clear about who you're targeting. These ideas aren't just helpful; they've helped reshape my business strategy and my mindset. Embracing these insights has deepened my commitment to daily growth, grounding me in a practice that fuels each new day with purpose. Every morning, I now start with gratitude, looking at each day as a chance to step up. This practice keeps me grounded and moving forward, ready to tackle the problems others might leave behind. In the end, it's this steady, daily commitment that fuels the journey.

11

The Road Ahead: A Patriot's Dream for America

Final Reflections: Embracing the Journey and Its Lessons

Getting out of your comfort zone might be very difficult, but when you do this, your brain will start to open up and you will see new opportunities you might have missed in the past. I was reading an interesting study and it shows that most heart attacks happen on Monday morning between 8 a.m. and 9 a.m. The research also showed 85% of Americans disliked their job and were not happy when they had to go to work. I guess that makes sense because if you have to do a job for years you really don't like, that could be very stressful. They get sick just thinking about it and it could literally kill them. One thing that I learned through the military and entrepreneurship is that you must get out of your comfort zone and meet like-minded people. It is great to have friends from childhood—that is extremely important. I have a handful of friends I have known over 25 years and we are extremely close. My recommendation is also to attempt to join a group of people trying to do the same thing you are. I did this while in the EO Accelerator which is for business owners making $250,000 to $1,000,000. It is a group of five of us and we have an accountability group. At first, I was nervous because I did not know anyone; however, I would have to be accountable to the group. I think this helps as a business owner because it gets lonely at times and, ultimately, you are going to be successful or you are not going to be. You have to be accountable for everything that goes on in the company because, at the end of the day, you sign the checks. Having the accountability, you are sharing all the dirty, nasty, grimy things that can happen in business and you are sharing best practices from people's personal experience. That is what I like about the group—no one is judgmental; they will just talk about their experience and maybe you might be able to get a nugget that could help you out with some of the issues you are facing

I heard a great quote that reads, "Life begins at the edge of your comfort zone." How I recognize that I am doing the right thing is that I feel the fear rushing into my body. Once I have that feeling, I know I must do the thing that is causing fear, such as reach out to a potential client that has not returned my phone calls. At first, I used to take it personally. Then I reprogrammed my thinking because I know that people are extremely busy. I know that our service can really help solve our customers' problems. I know many people that have problems with their cleaning services, and because we have a very solid system for hiring veterans and family members of veterans, we are successful. The teammates we hire already have values instilled in them through their service to our country. We also created a standard operating procedure booklet we give out to our team members. From those action items of finding the right team members and training them the way PCC operates, I am now more confident of our services and am sure we can meet our customers' needs. I challenge myself every day to meet new people because it scares me.

Build Your Tribe

One of the most important things I learned about business is people have to know who you are in order to buy your service or product. I think one of the biggest issues small business owners face is that they are unknown, so people can't buy their services. Believe me, I understand the challenges, especially at first starting with a very small budget.

The most important thing for me was focus. I had to focus my time, resources, and money into the place where I had the best chance of getting the biggest return on investment. After I would identify the best club, organization, or group, I would put a lot of time and energy into that group. As a kid, I learned you will get out of something what you put into it. For example, if you are a really good golfer and you put six hours a day into it, you can expect to play better because you are practicing. All those hours by yourself on the course will pay off in your games because you are putting the time in on the front end.

I think in the game of business, people are the most important thing. The more people whom you can come into contact with and whose interests are similar to yours, the better opportunity you have to be successful. You might have to challenge yourself and get out of your zip code to meet new people and I would totally encourage that. One thing that I learned is that I always want to shoot for the stars and meet people who are smarter and have more experience than I do in certain areas in life or business. Birds of a feather flock together so I want to find a strong tribe to be a part of. Try this; it will provide you the opportunity to learn new information and meet people that want to help you out. When I meet someone, I try to put myself in their shoes and figure out how I could help them out. It seems like if you try and help people out, things always work out for the best. I don't know about you, but it feels better to give than receive; how about you? However, if someone does give me a referral or something like that, I am very gracious. Here are a few principles that I have learned about meeting new people.

1. Practice your handshake and have a good grip. When you shake someone's hand, look them in the eyes while speaking. You are building a relationship. When you have a strong, firm handshake, it will tell people that you are confident in yourself.

2. Understand your footwork. If you are pointing your feet at the door and not at that person, people can tell through body language that you are not that interested. Point your feet towards them so that your words are matching your body language.

3. Speak up. Make sure that you speak up so people can hear what you are saying. In most networking events, there is always background noise. A little routine I do is speak in front of the mirror to myself before I go to an event to build confidence.

4. Last but not least, and probably the most important thing, is to smile and enjoy yourself. For the most part, if you are having fun and talking, you are a lot more approachable to people. Put on a smile and enjoy learning about other people.

One approach I used was to join an organization club that offers sports, such as basketball, tennis, squash, golf, swimming, and a lot of clubs. The clubs are pretty neat because they offer a wide variety of activities, such as business networking, speaking, whiskey and beer tasting, cards, singing, and many other activities. This takes time, but it is a really neat experience. You get to spend time with like-minded people that are challenging themselves and pushing hard to be a better person. What I have learned is that if you build a network of people that are positive and motivated, that will affect your state of mind and you will be more positive. If you want something different, do something different. That is a phrase I hear in my mind all the time from my mentor and friend Eric. I was going through a slump where it seemed like I could not get in contact with any of the decision makers and definitely not the people who made the final call. I also learned from other mentors it is easier to meet and work with top to bottom. I was not getting the results I wanted so I had to invest in something new. In entrepreneurship, you are always trying new things and learning from experience. The thing is that you have to learn quickly before you run out of money. PCC has been in business for seven years now and built a nice little nest egg. One thing that is very important though is to reinvest in the business. My thought process now is to reinvest in meeting the right people and to enjoy the company of new and exciting individuals.

See, Say, Work, Believe, Repeat

When I was working out this morning, some memories started flooding my brain about when I was a kid. Like I talked about earlier in the book, when I was a child, I was passionate about basketball. That got me thinking about how my past helped make me who I am today. When I would take a hot shower after practice and dry off, I would always write "Best at Basketball" on the mirror and say it to myself. I was probably a little superstitious, but I thought that would help me play better the next day. So I would see this and say this every day to myself for about 15 years. After that, I would work about five or six hours on my basketball game. Honestly, to me, it was not work because that was the one thing I was pretty good at, but all the practice really paid off on game days. I truly believed that I was the best at basketball. Were there better players than me? Of course there were. But in my mind, I was the best at basketball and I truly believed that. I think the most important thing is that no matter what anybody said about my game, I was internally very confident from seeing, saying, working, and believing.

The final step was to repeat the process so that I could come back the next day even better. I am going to explain how I used this when I was sick and also in business. When I was battling cancer, in the morning to myself, I would write *I am healing*. I would write this down every morning and see it with my own eyes and I could visualize it. The next step I would do is say *Waso*. As I had previously mentioned, I watched a video on Asian doctors who were trained on how to cure cancer. In the video, they were saying *Waso*. The meaning was "I am healing." I would walk and say this over and over again to myself. The next step was the work, so they cut the 25% of my right lung out. I could only walk a few minutes a day at first and had to build back my lung capacity. Then I had to do the four rounds of chemo, which was painful and a lot of work. The next thing I did was to believe that the treatment was really working and it totally did. I knew from experience that things would get worse before they got better. My mindset is that I knew this would be part of the process, but I believed each day I was getting better. I knew in my heart I would be okay and I truly internally believed that. The final step is repeat. I would repeat the steps each day and that will help me be successful because I have a system in place and know what my goals are.

The way I use this in business is to write my goal down so I can see it and then visualize it. For example, we will win a 45,000 sq ft contract in 45 days. I am going to write this goal down so that I can see it and write it down each morning, so it is fresh in my head. I will say this to myself a few times a day and remind myself of what I am working for. The next thing is I am going to work my butt off to make this happen. I will make 15 calls each day to qualified prospects. Then I will set up eight in-person meetings in one month. Then I will try to bid hopefully three or four buildings that month over 45,000 sq ft. That does not always happen, but at least I have my goals and a plan of action. Then, I truly believe in the work that we do at PCC. I have spent over seven years perfecting my craft and each day we get better from practice and experiment. Then I repeat this process. It is funny how I thought about this, but I have really been doing this in the past ten years and never knew. I am sure when you reflect on your life, you have systems put in place that work for you. Take some time and think about what has worked successfully for you in the past and try to implement it. I believe that the process I use could also work for you!

Seven Leadership Skills that Can Help Your Business

Just like a chef will follow their recipe to come up with the perfect dish, there are also ingredients that will help a business succeed. One of my mentors whom I listen to on YouTube is Bob Proctor. I have never met Mr. Proctor personally, but it really helps me think about my life and business when I listen to his podcast. I am going to list and explain the seven ingredients he speaks about to grow your business:

1. Set and achieve business goals. You have to be very clear when setting your goals. Most people don't set goals because they are afraid. I don't believe that is the right philosophy. When driving to a location, you must have a road map in order to get there, the same with business goals. You must set clear goals and then measure them. The worst-case scenario is you fail. If that happens, tweak something and try to improve. Practice makes perfect and at least you have a plan.

2. Maturation is going to be very important in your journey. You have to put the thing in your mind that makes you want to get out of bed in the morning and fight with passion. Life can be hard sometimes and you will not always want to get up and do the hard things. Your motivation on why you are doing it will help you achieve your goals.

3. Vision separates good managers from great leaders. Leaders have a vision and a plan to turn a small company into a medium and large-scale company. It is like the person has a blueprint in their mind and is very good at communicating the plan to the

rest of the team. It gets everyone excited so they have the energy and fortitude to keep pushing even when times get tough.

4. Courage is also a very important leadership trait because you are not guaranteed victory. You will be entering the unknown and you will have to face your fears. You are going to make decisions that will leave some people upset and others happy. You have to believe in yourself and follow your gut. This will take courage because people will try to sway you in the direction that possibly benefits them.
5. Integrity is another huge trait of leadership. You are only as good as your word—and if you don't do a good job, word of that will spread fast. You will have to make many tough calls, but if you have integrity, you will be money ahead. You will gain the respect of your peers and customers with your values.
6. Grit is one of the most important leadership skills you must have. Let me be clear—in life and business, you are going to get knocked down, beaten up, and bruised. The most important thing is to dust yourself off and get back into the fight. For me, sometimes this is easier said than done. I would rather just sit back and drink my coffee instead of calling a facility and explaining that I have to make a personnel change because that person cleaning is not paying attention to detail, shows up late to work too many times, or does not have the right type of mental attitude to be able to adapt to a changing environment. I know I will get some push back from the facility manager, but I need a team that is highly motivated to get the job done to the highest standards. I have learned the bigger you get, the more challenges you will face. That is why grit is so important, because you need to keep moving forward.

Live Every Day to the Fullest

The last thing I would like to talk about is living every day to the fullest. Sometimes you have to sit back and look at everything you have accomplished and take it all in. Life can be difficult sometimes, but it can also be awesome! I feel so fortunate to have my sons Tim Jr. and Tyler in my life. They are my legacy and I am so proud of them. It is going to be up to them to accomplish their dreams. I have 100% confidence in them and love them so much. I feel like the luckiest man alive to have married my best friend in the world Terri. We will be married 20 years this July 2024 and have been great friends for 27 years. If you can spend time with people that you love, you can accomplish anything. Thanks for reading *A Patriot's American Dream* and good luck with your dream!

12
To My Family

To Mom, Dad, Amy, and Aunt Mo

I just want to say thanks for being awesome parents and always being there for me and Amy. I love you guys more than words can say so this is why I had to write this book. I remember us getting up early Saturday mornings and we would watch the Big 8 sponsored by Phillips 66 before the Mizzou basketball game. Most of the Saturdays had two to three games that day, but that was always fun family time. Thanks for giving me the opportunity to do something I loved to do. I always appreciated your hard work ethic which you passed down to me. Both of you worked so hard and would sacrifice to give Amy and me the best possible outcomes. I know that I have always been a handful and probably worried you my whole life. I just had to do it my way; otherwise, I felt like I was cheating myself even though I am sure it was difficult on you at times. I always liked to call the shots and put my future into my own hands. Whatever happened would happen, but at least I was responsible for the outcome and it was on me. I always liked the excitement, and most likely that is why I joined the Army and became an entrepreneur. I just wanted to have a shot that I would not have had if I had not joined the Army. I loved working my ass off and choosing my own schedule. If I succeeded, it was on me or if I failed, it was on me.

Amy, I remember having bunk beds with you and me sleeping on the top bunk. Then we had the bedroom together when we lived with Grandma and Grandpa Smith. Time flies and it was always a good time. I remember us playing chugga chugga choo choo with our legs and eventually, it would turn into us just laughing and goofing off. You were always very good at school and the good kid, which I am sure made mom and dad's life a little easier when we were younger. Sorry you could not tell the teachers at Affton High School I was your brother because you were afraid that you would be judged because I was not the best high school student. You turned out to be a great mom and have an awesome family with Izzy, Benny, and Elliot, and I am happy for you and Adam. You have a great husband and I am so happy you two found each other and made a family together. I am very proud of you.

Aunt Mo, thanks for being my second mom and always being there for me. When I was younger, you took me everywhere and you always showed me a great time. Thanks for letting Terri, the kids, and me live with you. That really helped us out a lot and I am very appreciative. You were a great role model and that is one reason I got my social work degree—because I saw you care about people so much. You are an awesome aunt and I love you so much

To me, freedom is worth more than money. Money is definitely necessary because it provides me the options to focus on what I enjoy doing along with living longer since I pay for my medical insurance. Thanks for never giving up on me and realizing I would eventually find my own path.

To My Son Timmy

Hey, buddy! I love you so much and I am very proud of the young man you are becoming. I love how you are passionate about life and how you give 100% in anything in life that you do. You are my little warrior and can do anything you put your mind to. Life can be hard sometimes; that is when you have to bear down and keep moving forward. I loved coaching you in basketball and baseball and spending time with you when we were in the car driving to those events. You have a special talent in public speaking, and you draw people close to you. If you like the plumbing trade and learn enough about it, you will be in a great position by about 26 years old to open up your own shop. I am so glad you have been doing so well at Ranken Technical so far. You were blessed to be handy and you can work with your hands. You definitely got that from your mom and not me. One reason I think you can become a very successful business owner is because you are good at public speaking and voice that to many people at one time.

I believe in you and it is my honor to be your Dad. If you close your eyes, I will always be there for you and ready to listen. I can't wait to watch the man you become in the future and I will always be a part of you. Love you, buddy.

To My Son Tyler

Hey, Tati! I love you so much and you are turning into such a great young man. It has been a privilege for me to watch you grow over the years. I believe in you 100% and think that you can do whatever you pour your heart and soul into. I had a great time coaching you in basketball and hanging out with you and your friends during and after practice. The best part of it for me was honestly just spending time with you and having our conversations. Mom and I had a blast watching you play football as a kid. Honestly, that is why I love watching it now because I learned so much from watching you play.

One thing I notice about you is that you are a natural leader. When you do speak, people gravitate to you. The words you say connect with people and the other kids. You are great at saving money and have the right mindset when it comes to stacking your money. The most important life lesson I feel for you is to learn to sell and then back it up with your product. I know you can do that if that is what you really want to do. You are a lot like me where you will have to decide what you want to do. Somebody can suggest things to you, but you will have to make up your own mind that you want to do it. Remember, you are part of me, and my parents could tell me something over and over again but until I made the decision to do it, nothing really mattered. It will be up to you and I believe that you will find your passion one day. When life gets hard, please dig deep and find something that means everything to you. To be honest with you, without you, Timmy, and mommy, I don't know if I would have fought so hard to stay alive. You are everything to me. You are my Why and I love you buddy. Good luck in your future adventures and just know I will always be with you. Love you, buddy.

To My Beautiful Wife and My Best Friend Terri

Baby, wow, I can't even explain how much you mean to me and the boys.

The first time I saw you at the Oz on the Sunday Night Ritual, I had a gut feeling that you were the one for me. I remember when I got home that morning, I put your number in my shoe box underneath my bed so that I would not lose it.

I am so happy and fortunate we were best friends for six years before we got engaged and married. Those nights that we hung out together when we were younger meant a lot to me. I always thought we got each other when I did not think very many people got me. I always was very happy when I was hanging out with my friends and then you would join us. The nights when we did not meet up with each other, I remember giving you a call about 2 a.m. to page you and then we would have a great conversation before we went to bed. You were the only person I ever felt I could be vulnerable around. Having these conversations over the years is what made me really fall in love with you.

I remember when I enlisted in the Army, I really needed a change. It's funny how we started dating when I was in AIT and then we got engaged right before I was deployed to Iraq and then married after I returned home from Iraq. I did not want to get married before I went to Iraq because I did not know if I was going to make it home and wanted to save you from that type of hurt.

When I got home from Iraq, I remembered getting married at the courthouse because we only had 30 days before we had to move back to Germany, and it was an awesome experience that I was really pumped up about. For me to bring you over to Germany as a young man and travel the world with you is something I always remembered, and it provided me a new way at looking at life from traveling around the world.

You always believed in me and had my back and I really appreciated that—even when I resigned from my job and followed my dream of running Patriot Commercial Cleaning full-time. You are one in a million and you attract people to you because you are not only beautiful physically, but also as a person because you have a huge heart and care about people. I was fortunate enough to have two wonderful sons with you and so happy that we have such a tight-knit family, baby. You are a great mom and care so much about the boys. Sometimes, when I am out with them, they would tell me how lucky they feel to have you as their mom. You're my everything and my entire heart and I will love you until infinity.

A Q&A with Tim

Can you expand on your relationship with your parents during your high school years?

While I was in high school, I was always gone. I would be at the basketball courts or I would spend the night with my friends on the weekends. I would always call them to let them know I was going to be spending the night at a friend's house. My mom and dad would always say, "Make sure that you are careful." At that time, I was out running around with my buddies and I would not always make great decisions. I was living for the moment instead of looking to the future. I would say the relationship was strained sometimes because I was very hardheaded and would make up my own mind. Being parents, they only wanted the best for me, but a lot of the guys I grew up around were very street-smart and we were able to adapt to many environments. I learned to adapt to many different areas because if I hadn't, I would have really gotten taken advantage of. One thing I learned from going to the Boys Club of St. Louis at the age of eight was not to show weakness or be a punk. You better be able to stand up for yourself; otherwise, people will smell the fear on you and your life will become more difficult. Even if you fight and get whipped on, at least people knew you had heart and would throw down when you had to. When I was younger, my buddies and I looked out for each other because there was strength in numbers. I hung around many different types of people in high school—from hoosiers to nerds to Southside tough guys. I could go to many different parties and I was known a lot from being able to hoop. I was cool with a lot of different groups, which made my life easier. The hoosiers would always be on their skateboards at Mathilda park, skating around while we were hooping. I consider myself a hoosier because we always give each other shit and that's what we call each other. The nerds would help me out with my homework in high school, which I always appreciated because I did not give it my best sometimes and I just wanted to stay eligible. A lot of the Southside tough guys I knew since age eight going to the Club would call me up because I could hoop and help them when playing street games at different parks. They would look after me from knowing them so long, so a lot of people would not give me too much shit because of some of the guys I grew up with. So I grew up knowing a diverse group of people in high school and could get along with many different types of people from life experiences. My parents knew some of the guys I was hanging out with and just would shake their heads and tell me to be careful.

What specific incident made you realize basketball might not be your ticket out?

After playing at Forest Park Community College, my next stop was St. Mary's College in Leavenworth Kansas a D2 NAIA school. I was only there for six months. I started having problems with my feet from cutting so much. The bottom part on my foot my skin started peeling off and I would have to use a second skin to replace the real skin on my feet. I could not move as quick and in basketball, all you do is make cuts because it is a very fast-paced game. At that time, I knew I was going to lose my scholarship and be back home in St. Louis and that did happen. I transferred to UMSL while working different jobs for about 1.6 years. Basketball came to an end, and I was back in the same place. I knew if I ever wanted to see the world and make a life for myself, I was going to have to find another way. I felt stuck and I did not want to be that guy at the neighborhood bar talking about how I used to be able to play and now, ten years later, I'm stuck in the same place, telling the same story over and over.

How did your friends react to your decision to join the Army?

My buddies were all very supportive; they could see that I needed a change and wanted a fresh start. I think that it made some of them proud that I was trying something different and did not blame me for wanting something else in life. Of course, they would miss hanging out with me, but if there is one thing I know about St. Louis it's you could leave for four years and not much would change. Your buddies would continue working and would do whatever they were doing, but not much changes. I remember we had a lot of parties before I went to Basic Training, and we all had a great time. At the time, I was 24 years old and we were all living our best life. We were all getting by and would party pretty hard, but I'd say none of us at that time were looking ahead. I knew that I was not—I needed to see something new and was ready for the challenge.

Can you describe your emotions during your last day as a civilian?

I was like, "Damn I cannot believe that I am going into the Army and am about to have a Drill Sgt yelling at me, telling me what I can do and can't do." I tried to enjoy the last months of freedom before I knew that everything was going to change. I was going to be the last four digits of my social security number and not Tim anymore. I knew I needed discipline because basketball was the thing that always provided me with that. Now that it was gone, I had nothing else providing me with a schedule or anything that I really cared about. I was nervous about the future because I knew I was more than likely going into war. I felt like if I was going to go out, at least it would be honorable that I could bring pride to my family's name. I was enjoying my free time because I knew that the Army would have their own schedule for me, and I was going to be on their time. I was excited again and started working out hard about three months before I went in. I was part of the Delayed Entry Program, where the Army recruiter would take us new recruits to work out about three days a week. I started to get more focused, like when I was playing ball. I knew I had to get my body back in good shape—both mentally and physically for the challenges that were lying ahead of me.

Can you provide more details about your first day at basic training?

The first day of Basic Training I remember the Drill Sgts meeting us at the bus. We had to line up on the footprints and they greeted us by a little bit of yelling. It was 0300 in the morning. We bed down for a few hours and then we went into reception. We were there for about five days. There were a lot of people from all over the U.S. and from all different backgrounds. You had some guys who were about 18 years old and were talking shit from what state they were from. Remember, at this time, nobody had any type of military training and we were all a bunch of civilians. There was not much we could do in reception, so guys would be playing craps and cards because we were not in the Army yet. We were basically waiting to meet our Drill Sgts and get issued our uniforms, get the bald head, and all of the other drills that start once Basic Training begins. The first day on Basic Training after reception, they greeted us at the barracks—yelling, beating on drums, and throwing trash cans. Five drill Sgts would come up to you and start yelling to hurry up and throw you off however they could. It was a hot day in South Carolina in June 2003. Some of the soldiers had a tough time dealing with it and I think about three soldiers did not make it past the first two days; they were held and called hold-overs and would not complete Basic Training and not be able to adapt and receive some type of discharge. At first, it is overwhelming, but the Army has a saying that is very true: Hurry and wait. Over time, you get to know these soldiers. It has a lot to do with teamwork. You need to work with each other to overcome certain obstacles. Over time, you start to build strong bonds with one another because if one person messes up, everyone pays the consequences.

Can you provide more specific details about your initial PTSD symptoms?

When I first came back from the war in 2004 and my wife Terri was able to come over to Germany, we lived in military housing on the post. At night, I would wake up in a panic looking for my weapon because we had it with us 24-7. I would sometimes have very vivid dreams and Terri would have to let me know that I was at home and not deployed. I would have to wake up and just sit up on my bed for about 10 minutes before I could fall back asleep. I did not mention anything about this until the last two months when I knew I was going to be Honorably Discharged. Then I started getting some counseling, but I did not want to say anything while I was in the Army because I did not want it to affect my rank and it is something we never really talked about. At that time, we were in the middle of war and everyone on post was going through it. We would all just suck it up and drive on.

I remember July 2007 . . . we were staying at my Aunt Mo's on Arsenal St. A few blocks away was Berra park. All the fireworks brought back memories of all the outgoing star clusters at FOB St. Michaels and outgoing artillery with thunderous sounds of boom. I remember going into the basement and sit in a corner by myself just sobbing. All of these memories just flooded my brain and it felt like I was right back in Iraq. I knew I needed some counseling at the VA to help me get through this because it was a lot for me. Plus, I could not find work for six months after I got back home. I had too much time to think about things that I could not change.

How did your family react when you first told them about your cancer diagnosis?

My family was devastated when we first got the news. I was in shock because I never smoked before and just asked myself, "How did this happen?" My wife Terri was struggling because at the time Timmy Jr. was only 10 years old and Tyler was 8 years old. My Mom and Dad struggled with it very much and were definitely shaken. Overall, my family was very supportive throughout the entire journey. Some of the most joyful times were when I would beat the cancer, which I did three different times. At the same time, it is gut-wrenching when you get the news it is back. It is like your whole world just stops. You have to get ready to fight again and you know that you are going to have to go through hell to get the reward. At times, you have to do what you have to do. As long as there is a reward at the end, I never minded having to go through all the pain to come out healthy on the other side.

Looking back to the early days of Patriot Commercial Cleaning, were there moments when you felt like giving up?

I would say around 2021 and 2022; there were periods which were very hard for Patriot Commercial Cleaning. It was hard to find the right team members and people were not applying for jobs because of the pandemic.

What did you tell yourself in those moments to keep going?

I knew I had a family to support and would tell myself to keep driving on and pushing forward. This is how I provide for my family; therefore, I had to figure something out. Around 2024, it started to get a little better when it came to hiring the right team members. In those dark times you just have to stay focused and not give up. You have to try different strategies to make things work.

Throughout your journey, you've crossed paths with incredible people,

including a president, a governor, and countless others. But if you had to choose one person who left a lasting mark on you, who would it be—and why?

I would have to say my Dad made the biggest impression on me and is my hero. My dad was a very hard worker and took the time to coach my friends and me in basketball. He always taught me to never make excuses because, at the end of the day, it is up to you to provide for yourself and your family.

For veterans who might feel lost or unsure about their next steps, especially those who dream of starting a business, what words of wisdom would you offer?

I would say, "Look back to your military training. You have learned many transferable skills that you can apply in the civilian world. You learned how to adapt to many different environments and have worked with people all over the world. You have that never-quit spirit, even when facing daunting odds. You know how to act when you're under pressure. You have unique experiences that will help you stand out from your competition because of your military training. You have dealt with pressure because you were thrown into the fire—and you know how to take the pressure and become better because of it."

Captured Moments of Dedication and Honor

In the pages ahead, each image tells a story—not just of Tim's achievements, but of his unwavering dedication to service, resilience, and leading with purpose. From shaking hands with presidents and governors to receiving awards from members of Congress, these images showcase the recognition Tim has earned for his tireless work in business, veterans' advocacy, and community impact. Through national media interviews, military honors, and public celebrations, these moments of recognition are a testament to the countless lives Tim has touched along the way.

Tim with his wife, Terri

THE WHITE HOUSE

WASHINGTON

October 31, 2008

Sergeant Timothy J. Smith, USAR
5423 Arsenal Street
St. Louis, Missouri 63139

Dear Tim:

I was honored to meet you during my visit to St. Louis. I enjoyed my trip, and I appreciated your warm welcome.

Our country will never forget those who have served and sacrificed so that future generations may enjoy the blessings of liberty. I am grateful for your dedicated efforts to defend our way of life, and I am proud to be your Commander in Chief.

Thank you for the kind note. Best wishes, and may God bless you.

Sincerely,

George W. Bush

Letter to Tim from President George W. Bush

Roy Blunt
United States Senator

April 30, 2014

Mr. Timothy James Smith, Sr.
President
Patriot Commercial Cleaning
315 Lemay Ferry Road, Suite 107
St. Louis, MO 63125-1542

Dear Mr. Smith,

Congratulations on your recognition for the Veteran Small Business of the Year by the Small Business Administration.

Our nation's small businesses are the backbone of our economy and create half of all private sector jobs. I admire the sacrifice and hard work you've demonstrated in running a successful small business and employing your neighbors. Our communities thrive through the work of committed people like you, and your continued dedication makes Missouri an even better place to live and work. Keep up the good work.

I regret that the Senate schedule prevents me from being with you as you receive your award. Best wishes for the event and for continued success for your business.

Sincere regards,

Roy Blunt
United States Senator

NOT PRINTED OR PAID FOR AT TAXPAYERS EXPENSE

Letter to Tim from United States Senator, Roy Blunt

CLAIRE McCASKILL
MISSOURI

United States Senate
WASHINGTON, DC 20510

May 8, 2014

Mr. Timothy Smith Sr.
President
Patriot Commercial Cleaning
315 Lemay Ferry Rd Ste 107
Saint Louis, MO 63125-1542

Dear Mr. Smith,

It is my distinct pleasure to congratulate you on receiving the United States Small Business Administration's Veteran Small Business of the Year Award. You should be very proud of this accomplishment.

The work of local businesses, employees, and leaders like yourself in creating jobs and fueling economic growth is invaluable to the welfare of countless Missourians. By taking risks in order to provide new economic and employment opportunities, local businesses contribute enormously to the prosperity of our region and the betterment of our communities. Your work and dedication within the Missouri business community has benefited our region, state, and country.

Again, congratulations on receiving this award, and best wishes in all your future endeavors.

Sincerely,

Claire McCaskill
United States Senator

Letter to Tim from Senator Claire McKaskill

MAX CLELAND

November 8, 2008

Dear Tim:

I have heard about the work you are doing at the VA Center in St. Louis. I could not be more proud. I, too, know what it is like to have been wounded while serving my country. I also know that recovery involves much more than physical healing. Serving others plays an essential role. So, I admire not only your sacrifice but your brave decision to continue giving back to your community.

Your work at the VA assisting other veterans like yourself is truly an inspiration. It is citizen-leaders such as you that give me hope for our nation's future. With your example to guide us, we can overcome any obstacle and meet any challenge.

While your service in uniform may have been cut short, your service to our nation as a *Mission Continues* Fellow carries on. And, through it, you honor us all.

Sincerely,

Max Cleland

P.S. Proud of you!

Letter to Tim from Max Cleland

Wm. LACY CLAY
1st District, Missouri

COMMITTEES:
FINANCIAL SERVICES
Ranking Member,
SUBCOMMITTEE ON
DOMESTIC AND INTERNATIONAL
MONETARY POLICY
OVERSIGHT AND
GOVERNMENT REFORM
Member,
SUBCOMMITTEE ON
FEDERAL WORKFORCE,
U.S. POSTAL SERVICE AND THE CENSUS
Web Site: www.lacyclay.house.gov/

Congress of the United States
House of Representatives
Washington, DC 20515-2501

2418 Rayburn House Office Buildi
Washington, DC 20515
(202) 225-2406
(202) 226-3717 Fax

6830 Gravois Ave.
St. Louis, MO 63116
(314) 669-9393
(314) 669-9398 Fax

Thomas F. Eagleton U.S. Court Ho
111 S. Tenth Street, Suite 24.344
St. Louis, MO 63102
(314) 367-1970
(314) 367-1341 Fax

May 8, 2014

Mr. Timothy James Smith, Sr., President
Patriot Commercial Cleaning
315 Lemay Ferry Road, Suite 107
St. Louis MO 63125

Dear Mr. Smith:

I was pleased to learn of your being selected by the Small Business Administration to receive the 2014 Veteran Small Business of the Year Award.

This is a very prestigious honor and one which you richly deserve. The role of the small business is extremely important in helping our area to keep going and growing. It increases local employment, enriches the economy and creates a thriving, diverse and vibrant community. The invaluable vision and leadership that you have demonstrated in this most important area have enabled our city, state and region to grow and thrive.

Thank you so much for all that you have done to help others. Best wishes for every continued success in all of your future endeavors.

Sincerely,

Wm. Lacy Clay

Wm. Lacy Clay
Member of Congress

WLC:elm

Letter to Tim from member of Congress, Wm. Lacy Clay

CHIEF OF STAFF
UNITED STATES TRANSPORTATION COMMAND
508 SCOTT DRIVE
SCOTT AIR FORCE BASE IL 62225-5357

9 November 2022

Sergeant Timothy J. Smith, Jr., USA

Dear SGT Smith,

Thank you for your service to the Army. You serve as an exemplary model of the values and leadership expected from a "Soldier for Life". Your ongoing support of transititioning service members and your impact on Veteran organizations has not gone unnoticed. Your achievements speak of your continued hard work and dedication.

Congratulations on being awarded the Missouri Athletic Club's 2022 Veteran of Achievement Award.

Thank you for your service to our Nation and your continued support to Veterans and the community.

Soldier for Life!

Hooah! well done!

Sincerely

VINCENT B. BARKER
Major General, U.S. Army
Chief of Staff

Missouri Athletic Club's 2022 Veteran of Achievement Award Letter

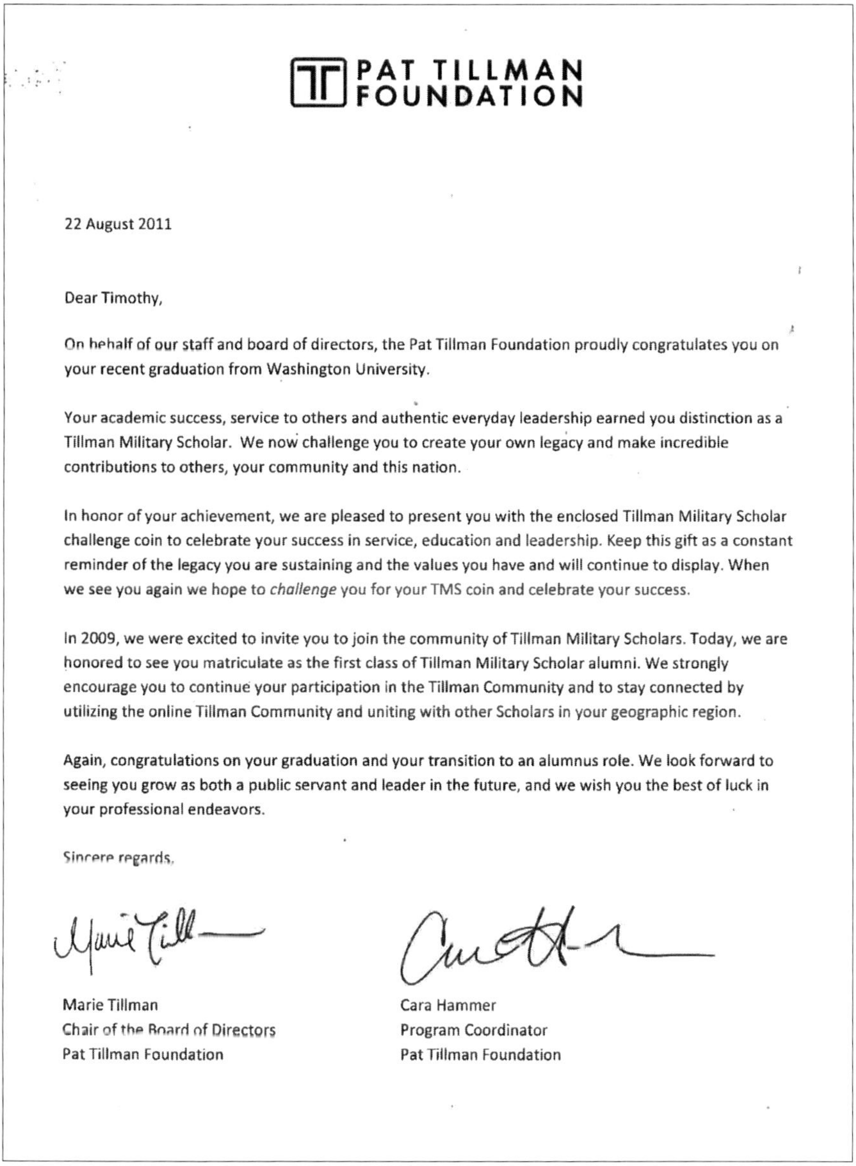

PAT TILLMAN FOUNDATION

22 August 2011

Dear Timothy,

On behalf of our staff and board of directors, the Pat Tillman Foundation proudly congratulates you on your recent graduation from Washington University.

Your academic success, service to others and authentic everyday leadership earned you distinction as a Tillman Military Scholar. We now challenge you to create your own legacy and make incredible contributions to others, your community and this nation.

In honor of your achievement, we are pleased to present you with the enclosed Tillman Military Scholar challenge coin to celebrate your success in service, education and leadership. Keep this gift as a constant reminder of the legacy you are sustaining and the values you have and will continue to display. When we see you again we hope to *challenge* you for your TMS coin and celebrate your success.

In 2009, we were excited to invite you to join the community of Tillman Military Scholars. Today, we are honored to see you matriculate as the first class of Tillman Military Scholar alumni. We strongly encourage you to continue your participation in the Tillman Community and to stay connected by utilizing the online Tillman Community and uniting with other Scholars in your geographic region.

Again, congratulations on your graduation and your transition to an alumnus role. We look forward to seeing you grow as both a public servant and leader in the future, and we wish you the best of luck in your professional endeavors.

Sincere regards,

Marie Tillman
Chair of the Board of Directors
Pat Tillman Foundation

Cara Hammer
Program Coordinator
Pat Tillman Foundation

Letter to Tim from the Pat Tillman Foundation congratulating him on graduating as a Tillman Military Scholar

Signed photo of Tim meeting Missouri Senator

Michelle Obama with Tim's family

THE ARCHITECT OF THE CAPITOL 1793

THE FLAG OF THE UNITED STATES OF AMERICA

This is to certify that the accompanying flag was flown over the United States Capitol on October 29, 2008.

At the request of the Honorable Wm. Lacy Clay, Member of Congress, this flag was flown to recognize Readen Clavier who has continued to serve the United States and his community through The Mission Continues Fellowship program. We honor your commitment to service and to your country.

Stephen T. Ayers, AIA
Acting Architect of the Capitol

2009-003884-007

Certificate of Flag Flown Over U.S. Capital

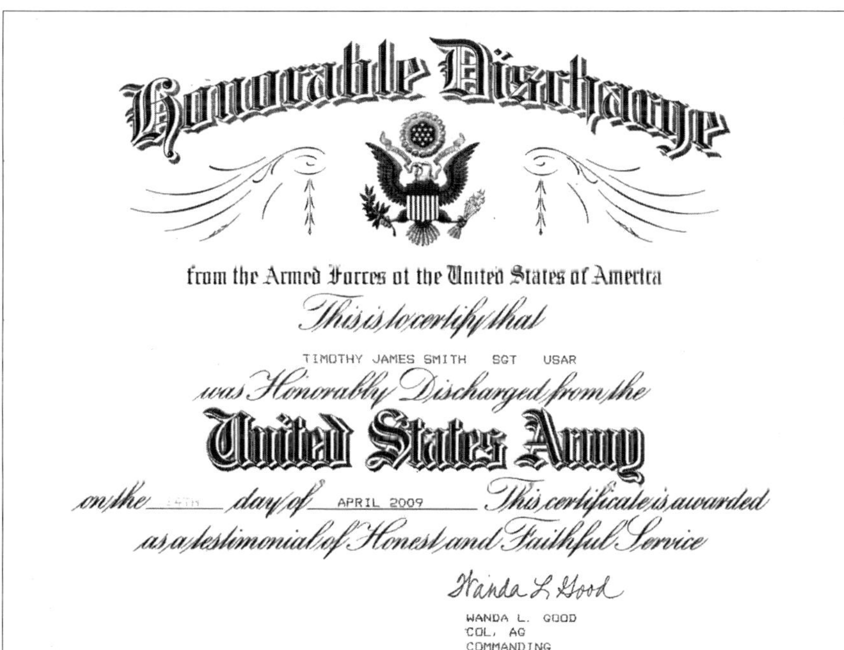

Honorable Discharge

from the Armed Forces of the United States of America

This is to certify that

TIMOTHY JAMES SMITH SGT USAR

was Honorably Discharged from the

United States Army

on the 14TH day of APRIL 2009 This certificate is awarded as a testimonial of Honest and Faithful Service

WANDA L. GOOD
COL, AG
COMMANDING

Honorable Discharge Certificate April 14, 2009

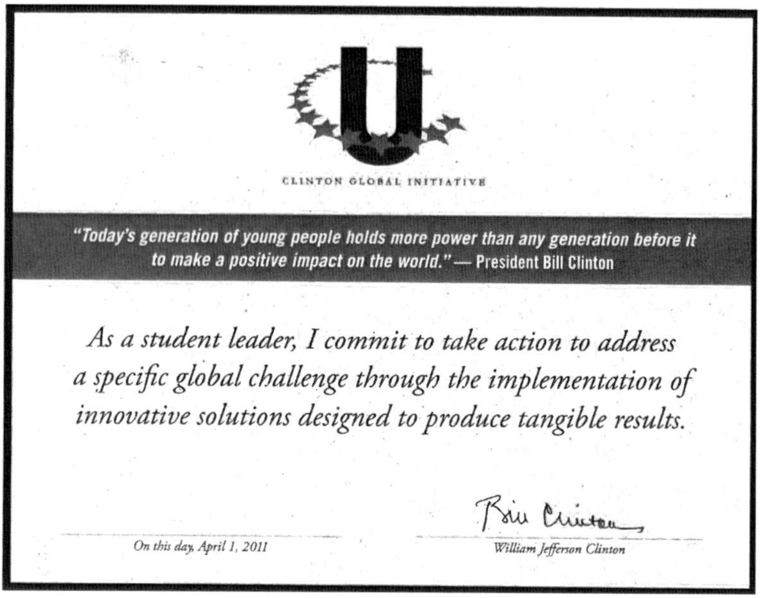

CLINTON GLOBAL INITIATIVE

"Today's generation of young people holds more power than any generation before it to make a positive impact on the world." — President Bill Clinton

As a student leader, I commit to take action to address a specific global challenge through the implementation of innovative solutions designed to produce tangible results.

On this day, April 1, 2011

William Jefferson Clinton

Clinton Global Initiative Student Leader

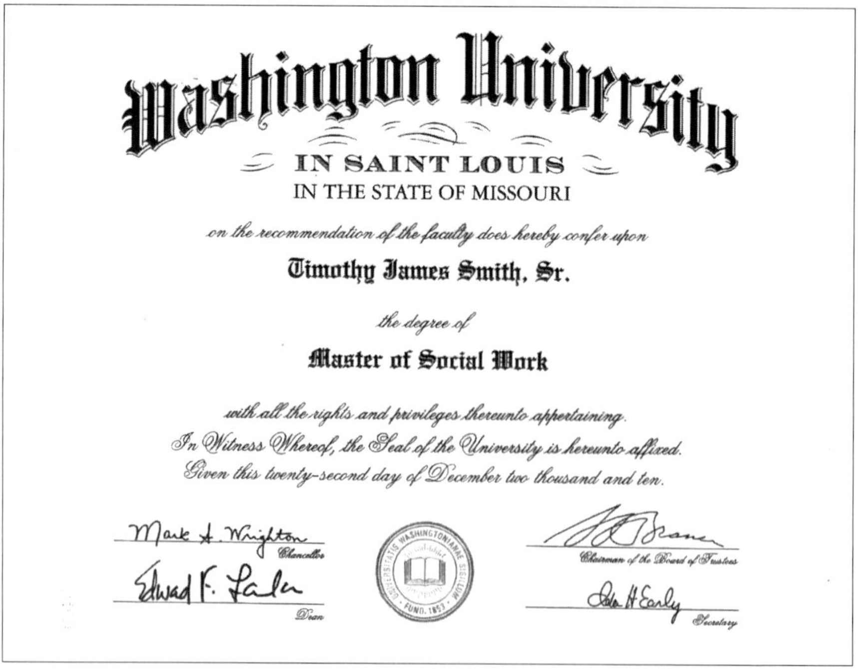

Washington University

IN SAINT LOUIS

IN THE STATE OF MISSOURI

on the recommendation of the faculty does hereby confer upon

Timothy James Smith, Sr.

the degree of

Master of Social Work

with all the rights and privileges thereunto appertaining.
In Witness Whereof, the Seal of the University is hereunto affixed.
Given this twenty-second day of December two thousand and ten.

Chancellor

Dean

Chairman of the Board of Trustees

Secretary

Washington University Master of Social Work Degree

Tim on Inc. Magazine Cover 2012

STREET SMARTS

Norm Brodsky

Service Above and Beyond

Military entrepreneurs have a higher calling, and we can all learn something from that

TIM SMITH IS AN ARMY VETERAN who served in Iraq. He saw combat there, lost eight friends in a horrific truck bombing, and returned home with posttraumatic stress disorder. His PTSD gave him night terrors and impeded his ability to reconnect with his wife and their two young sons. He was also unemployed for six months, which made it even more difficult for him to put the war behind him.

But he fought back. He did it by refocusing on service to others. After earning his master's degree in social work, he began working with veterans facing challenges like his. His desire to help them led him to start a business, Patriot Commercial Cleaning. Its mission: to provide jobs for returning service members and their family members, while delivering superior service to the company's commercial customers. By the time I met Tim, the business was established and growing. The most pressing question he posed was whether to accept an offer from a holding company to purchase 49 percent of his business.

Nothing I've worked on recently has been more rewarding than the opportunities to mentor military entrepreneurs like Tim. Veterans, reservists, and spouses of active-duty service members have been starting businesses like crazy over the past five years. In 2011, *Inc.* launched a program to support them, including mentoring by Inc. 5000 entrepreneurs. I was fortunate to be involved.

These are not your typical entrepreneurs. What you notice first are their impeccable manners. It's all "yes, sir" and "thank you, sir" and "here's what I'd appreciate your advice on, sir." You know immediately that you're dealing with people who are deeply grateful for your help, which naturally makes you want to help them even more.

They face unique challenges. Imagine starting a business and factoring in not only all the usual considerations but also the possibility that you might have to pick up and move far away on a moment's notice. Yet they are undaunted—because they have a higher calling. Like Tim, most of them are in business to help other military people and their families. Sure, they want to make money, but mainly they want to support their peers.

That said, Tim couldn't help being tempted by the offer from the holding company. I suggested that, before deciding whether to accept it, he and his wife, Terri, should talk about what was most important to them and where they wanted to be—in life and in business—10 years from now. When they did, they realized that their highest priority was to continue providing jobs for returning veterans and their spouses. "When I was out of work, my PTSD was worse because I had too much time to think about the past," Tim said. "Our mission is to help veterans out, be a part of a team again. If I'm independent, I can make sure we stay focused on that." He turned the offer down.

At my suggestion, Tim and Terri also put together a seven-year life plan, including a list of goals detailing what they want out of their lives, right down to the number of vacation days they want to take as a family. That was a life-changing experience, Tim said. I guess that makes us even. Working with Tim and the other military entrepreneurs has been a life-changing experience for me.

Norm Brodsky is an Army veteran as well as a veteran entrepreneur. His co-author is editor-at-large Bo Burlingham. They also are co-authors of *Street Smarts: An All-Purpose Tool Kit for Entrepreneurs*. Follow them on Twitter at *@normbrodsky* and *@boburlingham*.

FVAN KAFKA

SCAN THE PAGE TO SEE NORM ANSWER ANOTHER QUESTION FROM AN ENTREPRENEUR. (See page 12 for details.)
Do you have a question for Norm? Write to him at *AskNorm@inc.com*.

Inc. Magazine Feature Article, March 2014

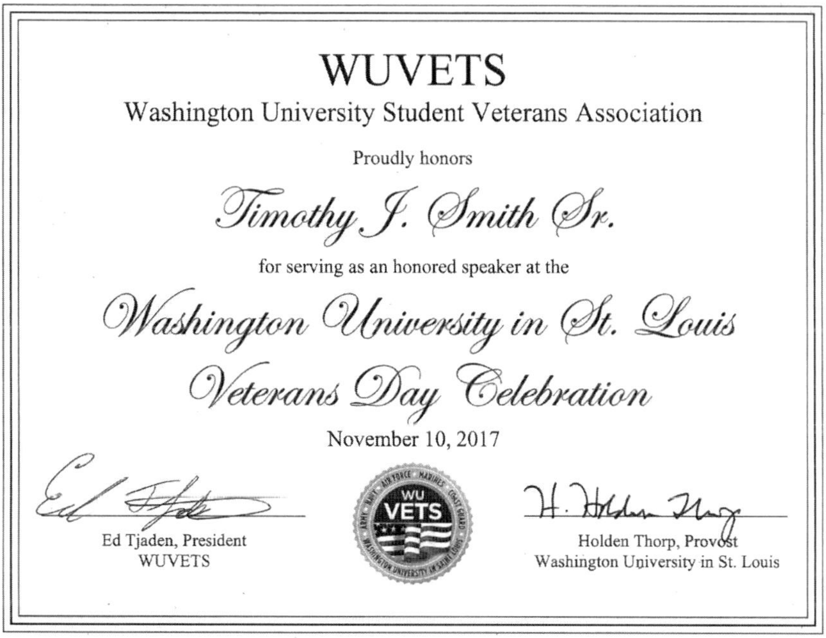

WUVETS

Washington University Student Veterans Association

Proudly honors

Timothy J. Smith Sr.

for serving as an honored speaker at the

Washington University in St. Louis

Veterans Day Celebration

November 10, 2017

Ed Tjaden, President
WUVETS

Holden Thorp, Provost
Washington University in St. Louis

Washington University Student Veterans - Honored Speaker

VA ST. LOUIS HEALTHCARE SYSTEM
VOCATIONAL SERVICES

VOCATIONAL SERVICES

Certificate of Appreciation

AWARDED TO

Tim Smith, President

Patriot Commercial Cleaning

To recognize your participation and support in creating a cultural shift to capitalize on Veterans' strengths in employment.

Jay Mendell,
Vocational Services Supervisor
VA St. Louis Health Care System

VA St. Louis Healthcare System Vocational Services Award

[the mission continues]
Center for Citizen Leadership

The Center for Citizen Leadership recognizes

Timothy Smith

for continuing his service to the United States through *The Mission Continues* Fellowship Program

November 8, 2008

Eric Greitens
Chairman

Kenneth Harbaugh
Executive Director

The Mission Continues Fellowship Program

Certificate of Achievement

Presented To

SGT Timothy Smith

23 February 2006

For outstanding achievement in selection as the 1st Armored Division Noncommissioned Officer of the Quarter (2d Qtr, FY06). Your commitment to duty and excellence reflect the true spirit of "Old Ironsides". Your significant contributions to the 2d Brigade Combat Team serves as an example for all to emulate and reflects great credit upon yourself, the 1st Armored Division, and the United States Army.

MICHAEL S. TUCKER
Brigadier General, US Army
Acting Commander

Certificate of Achievement 1st Armored Division

On behalf of Missouri's Veterans, the Governor of the Great State of Missouri presents the

SHOW-ME HEROES

FLAG OF FREEDOM AWARD

This subdued U.S. Flag patch was worn in a combat theater by a Missouri National Guardsman.

This certificate is awarded to

Patriot Commercial Cleaning LLC

in recognition of its promotion of excellence in Missouri's workforce by reaching out to, and employing, Missouri's Veterans and members of our National Guard and Reserve.

Director, Show-Me Heroes Michelle Matthews	October 7, 2015 Date	Governor Jeremiah W. (Jay) Nixon

12808

Show-Me Heroes Flag of Freedom Award

A15

SATURDAY OCTOBER 4, 2008

ST. LOUIS POST-DISPATCH

STLTODAY.COM

M 1

President George W. Bush congratulates St. Louisan Eric Greitens after honoring Greitens, of the Center for Citizen Leadership, and Timothy Smith (center) and Michael Boyd, volunteers with the VA Hope Recovery Center, following his arrival Friday at Lambert-St. Louis International Airport.
John L. White
Post-Dispatch

President appears on behalf of Hulshof

3y Jo Mannies
OST-DISPATCH
OLITICAL CORRESPONDENT

resident George W. Bush made a short top in St. Louis County on Friday to help aise $1.5 million for fellow Republican enny Hulshof, one of several signs that he national GOP is paying closer attenion to the state.

Republican National Committee Chairnan Robert M. "Mike" Duncan also was n the area Friday to attend the fundraiser nd to encourage volunteers at the party's oint campaign headquarters in Maryland Heights.

"Missouri is a target state," Dunan said in a brief telephone interview. You're going to see an RNC presence ere until Election Day. We're doing very vell here."

He discounted recent polls, including everal for the Post-Dispatch, that show Iulshof trailing Democratic opponent ay Nixon and Democratic presidential andidate Barack Obama about even gainst Republican John McCain.

Analysts and many activists in both najor parties say McCain must carry Missouri to win the White House.

McCain's campaign indicated as nuch earlier this week, when leaders nnounced that his campaign was with-

ST. LOUISAN GETS HONOR

President George W. Bush presented the President's Volunteer Service Award to Eric Greitens during his visit to St. Louis Friday.

Greitens, a lieutenant in the Navy Reserve and a Navy SEAL, started the Center for Citizen Leadership after returning from active duty that took him to Iraq, Afghanistan, Africa and Southeast Asia. The St. Louis-based nonprofit, which Greitens started with his combat pay and help from two friends, helps wounded and disabled soldiers pursue careers in public service.

Greitens, a Parkway North High School graduate, lives in St. Louis.

---

in Missouri. The latest figures by TNSMI-Campaign Media Analysis Group, a nonpartisan firm monitoring TV ad spending for the Post-Dispatch, showed Obama spending at least $369,035 on ads airing in Missouri last week, compared with $115,752 for McCain. The Republican was running ads only in St. Louis and Kansas City, while Obama's ads were airing statewide.

Duncan said he was heartened by the

Follow the money

STLtoday.com/info

In our searchable database, check out the Missouri and Illinois residents who have been giving money to the presidential candidates.

with the Democratic running mate, Joe Biden, at Washington University. Duncan said the rally turnout underscored his confidence that Missouri will go for McCain.

"The people of Missouri match up with the values of the McCain-Palin ticket," Duncan said.

Missouri Democratics disagree. On Friday, the party and labor launched the first of several events in the coming days aimed at highlighting the plight of area workers who have lost jobs.

"They're shipping our jobs to Canada, and we've heard nothing from the Bush administration," said Joe Shields, president of United Auto Workers Local 110. Shields expects to lose his job soon as a result of Chrysler's decision to curb production at one Fenton plant and close another by Oct. 31.

Hulshof was accompanying Bush on Air Force One. Hulshof spokesman Scott Baker said the congressman was thrilled

President Bush St. Louis Post-Dispatch newspaper article, October 4, 2008

Signed photo to Tim from President George W. Bush

Small Business Week Eastern Missouri cover photo, May 2014

SMALL BUSINESS WEEK WINNERS

Veteran-Owned Small Business of the Year

Timothy James Smith Sr., President
Patriot Commercial Cleaning

Tim Smith, a former Army Sergeant and Operation Iraqi Freedom Veteran, founded Patriot Commercial Cleaning in 2011 in order to help fellow Veterans and their family members. Patriot Commercial Cleaning only hires Veterans and their family members, currently 19 employees, to clean office spaces and schools. His goal is to have Veterans gainfully employed and to feel as if they are part of a team again.

He received assistance from the Veterans Business Resource Center (VBRC) to achieve his dream of helping fellow Veterans. Tim was featured at the Inc 500/5000 award ceremony in 2011.

In 2008, he was the first Missouri Mission Follows Fellow where he was personally recognized by President George W. Bush, is the Founder and Chairman of Stand United for Veterans at Washington University in St. Louis, and is the recipient of an award from Work Vessels for Veterans.

He currently raises money for ProNet International Gifts and Scholarships, mentors other Veterans in Mission Continues, and speaks to potential small business owners in the VBRC.

2014 SMALL BUSINESS WEEK
OF EASTERN MISSOURI

Small Business Week Eastern Missouri - Veteran-Owned Small Business of The Year

Entrepreneurial Business of the Year

Timothy Smith

Patriot Commercial Cleaning, LLC

When Timothy Smith, an Operation Iraqi Freedom veteran, was honorably discharged from the Army in 2007, he couldn't find a job for six months. Struggling with having no purpose and a diagnosis of PTSD, he had too much time to think about things he could not change. That's when he decided to start Patriot Commercial Cleaning to help other veterans. "I really enjoy working with the veteran community, and I have a new sense of purpose," he says. "My new mission is to hire team members that have the same values that we do and provide the best cleaning and customer service to the facilities that we clean."

Smith's business has grown to include nightly janitorial cleaning as well as striping and waxing floors and extracting carpet for private schools, buildings for property managers, day cares and any other facilities that are between 15,000 and 350,000 square feet. While he has grown his business, Smith's focus has remained on providing opportunity and purpose to fellow veterans.

"Being a veteran myself, it is very important for me to try and hire as many veterans that I can to be a part of a team again," he says. "I work very closely with the Department of Veterans Affairs vocational rehab specialist so we can put these men and women back to work. We have so we have built a very good track record. Our team members have been trained to take pride in our work and have very high standards. Those values are a huge asset to Patriot Commercial Cleaning because it is all about having the right company culture."

Earning the Entrepreneurial Business of the Year Award is a huge accomplishment for Patriot Commercial Cleaning and Smith. "It helps us know that we are going in the right direction and that people really care for the veteran community and want to see us succeed," says Smith. "This is a benchmark for us to let us know we are going in the right direction. There is still a lot of work to do, but I am having a

2018 Small Business Monthly Entrepreneurial Business of The Year Award

ABOVE & BEYOND

FY2007

CERTIFICATE OF APPRECIATION

PRESENTED TO

TIMOTHY SMITH

ST. LOUIS P & DC – TOUR ONE

An official commendation and recognition of your contributions to the United States Postal Service

DECEMBER 7, 2007

DATE

DEBRA REEVES
SENIOR MDO – TOUR ONE

Above and Beyond Special Recognition

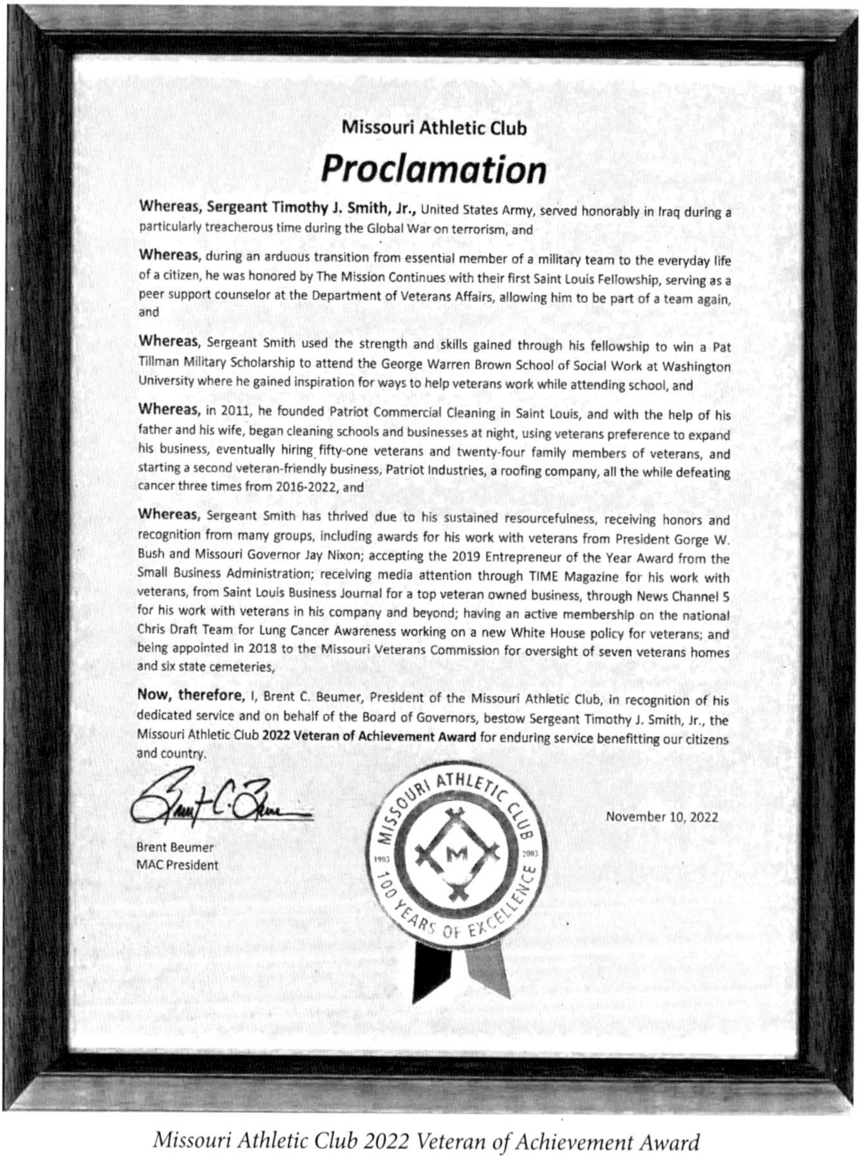

Missouri Athletic Club

Proclamation

Whereas, Sergeant Timothy J. Smith, Jr., United States Army, served honorably in Iraq during a particularly treacherous time during the Global War on terrorism, and

Whereas, during an arduous transition from essential member of a military team to the everyday life of a citizen, he was honored by The Mission Continues with their first Saint Louis Fellowship, serving as a peer support counselor at the Department of Veterans Affairs, allowing him to be part of a team again, and

Whereas, Sergeant Smith used the strength and skills gained through his fellowship to win a Pat Tillman Military Scholarship to attend the George Warren Brown School of Social Work at Washington University where he gained inspiration for ways to help veterans work while attending school, and

Whereas, in 2011, he founded Patriot Commercial Cleaning in Saint Louis, and with the help of his father and his wife, began cleaning schools and businesses at night, using veterans preference to expand his business, eventually hiring fifty-one veterans and twenty-four family members of veterans, and starting a second veteran-friendly business, Patriot Industries, a roofing company, all the while defeating cancer three times from 2016-2022, and

Whereas, Sergeant Smith has thrived due to his sustained resourcefulness, receiving honors and recognition from many groups, including awards for his work with veterans from President Gorge W. Bush and Missouri Governor Jay Nixon; accepting the 2019 Entrepreneur of the Year Award from the Small Business Administration; receiving media attention through TIME Magazine for his work with veterans, from Saint Louis Business Journal for a top veteran owned business, through News Channel 5 for his work with veterans in his company and beyond; having an active membership on the national Chris Draft Team for Lung Cancer Awareness working on a new White House policy for veterans; and being appointed in 2018 to the Missouri Veterans Commission for oversight of seven veterans homes and six state cemeteries,

Now, therefore, I, Brent C. Beumer, President of the Missouri Athletic Club, in recognition of his dedicated service and on behalf of the Board of Governors, bestow Sergeant Timothy J. Smith, Jr., the Missouri Athletic Club **2022 Veteran of Achievement Award** for enduring service benefitting our citizens and country.

Brent Beumer
MAC President

November 10, 2022

Missouri Athletic Club 2022 Veteran of Achievement Award

2008

Veterans Day Celebration

Honoring

THE MISSION CONTINUES FELLOWS

Saturday,

November 8, 2008

St. Louis City Hall

About the Fellows

SONIA MENESES — ARMY, 1996 - 2008

Sonia was a heavy wheeled vehicle operator, and is a graduate of the U.S. Army Air Assault School, and a member of the Audie Murphy Club. She deployed on two combat tours to Iraq and drove in ground convoys. Weapons fire and explosions caused significant hearing loss. Other symptoms, including loss of consciousness, required her medical evacuation. Eventually, Sonia was diagnosed with Ménière's Disease.

As a *Mission Continues* Fellow, she serves as a volunteer and mentor at Big Brothers Big Sisters of Clarksville, Tenn.

MICHAEL PAUL — ARMY, 1990 - 1994

Michael served during Operations Desert Shield and Desert Storm., attended Ranger school, and was assigned to an elite long range reconnaissance and surveillance unit. Michael suffered a spinal chord injury in a parachuting accident, but has since become a competitive wheelchair athlete. He is pursuing his Masters degree in Human Service and Counseling.

As a *Mission Continues* Fellow, Michael worked on his certification as a professional adaptive alpine skiing instructor and worked with the National Sports Center for the Disabled (NSCD) and Wounded Warrior Clinics.

ALICIA PRIBADI — MARINE CORPS, 2000 - 2005

Alicia worked as a Motor Transportation Operator and an Indonesian Translator in the Marine Corps. She was on the scene in the aftermath of the Sept. 11 attack on the Pentagon, and pulled charred materials from the structure for the following year. Alicia has been diagnosed with asthma and back injuries, and was medically retired from the Marines in 2005.

Alicia suffers from fibromyalgia, which prevents her from maintaining regular employment. As a *Mission Continues* Fellow, she started a fibromyalgia support group in Honolulu and partnered with the O'ahu Vet Center to begin group meetings.

TIMOTHY SMITH — ARMY, 2003 - 2007

Timothy deployed with a field artillery unit to Iraq in 2004. Upon his return to the United States, Tim was diagnosed with Post Traumatic Stress Disorder and a severe eye condition.

As a *Mission Continues* Fellow, Tim volunteered at the Dept. of Veterans Affairs as a peer counselor and was hired on full-time. Tim attends Washington University and is pursuing an MSW with a focus on mental health issues. He continues to serve as Veterans Outreach Coordinator for the St. Louis area.

MATHEW TROTTER — NAVY, 1999 - 2007

Mathew was an Aviation Technician and deployed multiple times during the War on Terror. He was seriously injured while serving and has undergone six reconstructive surgeries.

As the Travis Manion *Mission Continues* Fellow, Mathew worked with the Triple H Equitherapy Center in Texas, and was eventually hired on full-time. He built an equine therapy program to assist other wounded veterans with their recovery. Mathew also trains others to serve as mentors for troubled youth engaged in service programs at Triple H.

The Mission Continues Fellows

Tim in Iraq in 2004

Welcome Home Tim sign

Robert Troutt
Humanitarian Award
Presented To

Timothy J. Smith Sr.

In Appreciation Of Your Military Service
And In Acknowledgement Of Your Continued
Acts Of Service To Military Veterans

Presented by the Board of
ProNet International Gifts & Scholarships,
Assisting Veterans And Their Families
May 7, 2011

ProNet International Gifts & Scholarships
The Charitable Arm Of
ProNet International, Inc.

President Vice-President

Robert Trout Humanitarian Award

Tim cleaning in 2011

Workers of Patriot Commercial Cleaning

About the Author

Timothy J. Smith Sr. is a man who has lived the kind of life that movies are made of—a life marked by loss, resilience, and an unbreakable will to serve. Born and raised in St. Louis, Missouri, Tim's early years were spent more on the basketball court than in classrooms, as he sought his place in a world that didn't always make sense. In 2003, he made a decision that would alter the course of his life forever: he enlisted in the U.S. Army, a choice driven by the desire to serve something greater than himself.

Tim's journey took him to Iraq in 2004, where he faced the unthinkable. He witnessed the brutal realities of war, lost friends on the battlefield, and experienced bonds with fellow soldiers that were forged in fire and loss. Those experiences left scars—both visible and invisible. Coming home, he carried the weight of PTSD, fighting battles that only those who have been to war can understand. Yet, through the darkness, Tim found light in the unyielding support of his community and a newfound purpose in serving others.

When he returned home, Tim turned to education with a passion that defied his younger years. He earned a master's degree in Social Work from Washington University in St. Louis and was honored as a Pat Tillman Military Scholar—a recognition that spoke not only to his service but to his drive to lead. But his journey didn't end there; it only evolved. Tim transformed his pain into purpose, founding Patriot Commercial Cleaning, a business built to give back by creating opportunities for his fellow veterans. It was more than a company; it was a mission, one that would employ those who had served and struggled to find their way home.

Throughout his life, Tim has met some of the most powerful figures in the nation, from presidents to governors. Yet, it was the everyday heroes—his brothers and sisters in arms—who left the deepest impact on him. They inspired him to keep going, even when life threw him curveballs that would have broken most people. In addition to PTSD, Tim faced down another formidable enemy: cancer. Not once, but multiple times. Each diagnosis was a new battle, but he faced every single one with the same courage and determination that had carried him through war.

Tim is a devoted husband and father to two sons, a successful entrepreneur, and a fierce advocate for veterans. His work with the Department of Veterans Affairs as a peer support counselor and his founding of Stand United for Veterans have allowed him to touch countless lives. He's also deeply involved with organizations like The Mission Continues, where he mentors and inspires others to overcome their own struggles and find purpose.

Tim's story is more than an inspiring tale; it's a testament to the power of human resilience. In *A Patriot's American Dream*, he invites readers into his journey, sharing the raw and real experiences that shaped him. His life is a call to action—for anyone who has ever faced loss, felt lost, or needed a reminder that even in our darkest hours, we can find purpose. Tim's legacy is one of strength, service, and the belief that, no matter what life throws at us, there is always a way forward.

The following two pages show distinguished organizations and authorities who've recognized Tim's transformative impact and achievements.

FOX 2 now

MISSOURI ATHLETIC CLUB
M
Est. 1903

PAT TILLMAN FOUNDATION

ST. LOUIS SBM Small Business Monthly
The Source for Business Owners

CLINTON GLOBAL INITIATIVE

Missouri Department of Economic Development

THE MISSION CONTINUES
Reporting for Duty in Your Community

MISSOURI VETERANS COMMISSION